TRIUMPH

BONNEVILLE AND TR6

TIMOTHY REMUS

1961 TRI. T120

MBI Publishing Company

First published in 2000 by MBI Publishing Company,
729 Prospect Avenue, PO Box 1, Osceola, WI
54020-0001 USA

MBI Publishing Company books are also available at
discounts in bulk quantity for industrial or sales-pro-
motional use. For details write to Special Sales
Manager at Motorbooks International Wholesalers &
Distributors, 729 Prospect Avenue,
PO Box 1, Osceola, WI 54020-0001 USA.

Library of Congress Cataloging-in-Publication Data

Remus, Timothy
    Triumph Bonneville and TR6/Timothy Remus.
        p. cm.—(Motorcycle color history)
    Includes index.
    ISBN 0-7603-0665-6 (pbk.: alk. paper)
    1. Triumph motorcycle—History. I. Title.
    II. Motorbooks International motorcycle
        color history.
TL448.T7 R46   2000
629.227'5'0941—dc21   00-027081

On the front cover: The Bonneville first arrived in
America in 1959. This 1959 model and the ones to
follow had a combination of sterling engine
performance, superlative handling, and refined style
that changed the motorcycle scene in America forever.

On the frontispiece: Amal carbs provided carburetion
throughout most of the Bonneville's life span. This
single Amal 376 graces a 1962 TR-6.

On the title page: This rare 1961 T120C uses high
pipes running along either side of the bike. Note the
smaller TR6-style gas tank and "radiator grille" tank
badge. While the C stood for competition, these bikes
were street legal—unlike the later TT models.

On the back cover: *Top:* This 1967 TT bike is the work
of restorer Rick Brown. A painter by trade, the bike is
detailed to the max and is also very correct. The
Aubergine (purple) and gold paint job on the gas tank
is Rick's own. *Bottom:* Dusty Copage sails off the jump at
the Ascot TT. *Walt Mahoney*

Edited by Paul Johnson
Designed by John L. Sticha

Printed in Hong Kong

Contents

Acknowledgments 7

Introduction 9

CHAPTER 1: Triumph's High-Performance Saga Begins
The Speed Twin and Thunderbird 11

CHAPTER 2: The Right Bikes at the Right Time
The Bonneville and TR-6 23

CHAPTER 3: The Legend is Launched
A Bonneville Built for America 33

CHAPTER 4: Conquering the Competition
The TT Specials and C Bikes 53

CHAPTER 5: In a League of Their Own
The Bonneville and TR-6 Racers 67

CHAPTER 6: A Refined Sportbike
The Production Bonneville Evolves 87

CHAPTER 7: A Radical Redesign Goes Wrong
The Oil-In-Frame Bonnevilles 103

CHAPTER 8: The Bonneville Falls Behind
Triumph Closes Its Doors 117

Epilogue
An Icon Rises from the Ashes 125

Index 128

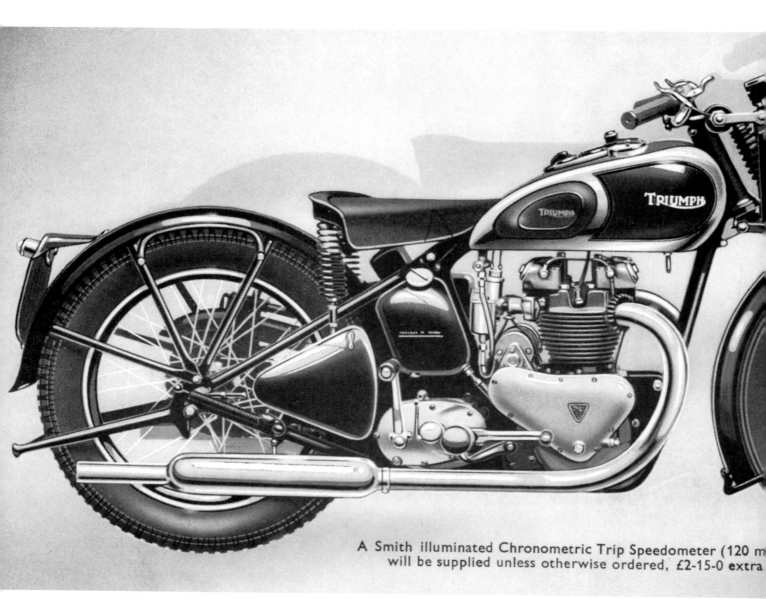

A Smith illuminated Chronometric Trip Speedometer (120 m
will be supplied unless otherwise ordered, £2-15-0 extra

Most of us focus on the later Triumphs: the T110, TR6, and Bonneville (the sex machines of their day). Lost in the nostalgic haze is the Speed Twin, the vertical twin that set the pattern for all the Triumph twins to follow. *Dick Brown collection*

CHAPTER I

Triumph's High-Performance Saga Begins

The Speed Twin and Thunderbird

A good story needs a beginning and an end. The nonfiction account of the Bonneville and TR6, certainly one of the more interesting and long-lived sagas to come out of motorcycling, is no different. In this case the history starts not with the first Triumph or the first Bonneville, but with a certain very notable vertical twin introduced to the world in 1937.

At a time when most motorcycles were either thumper singles or heavy, sidecar-lugging Fours or V-twins, Triumph introduced their new 500-cc vertical twin, dubbed the Speed Twin.

Restored by Gary Chitwood for Bobby Sullivan, this T100 dates from 1948. The silver sheen color first used on the prewar Tiger singles helped to separate the T100 from the very similar Speed Twin. Chrome-plated rims measure 19 inches on both ends.

A twin-cylinder Tiger 100 up against an earlier Tiger 90 single-cylinder Triumph from 1937. Note the similarities and the shared parts between the two bikes.

The genius credited with the design and birth of the new twin is Edward Turner. Originally a designer for Ariel Motorcycles, Turner joined Triumph when that company came under the ownership of Jack Sangster. The Sangster family owned controlling interest in Ariel for many years, though Jack took on more day-to-day responsibility for the motorcycle business when Ariel began to suffer from the effects of the Depression in the early 1930s.

Edward Turner came to Ariel in 1928, and immediately set about designing the Ariel Square Four. A revolutionary machine at the time, not only were the cylinders arranged in a square, the valves were operated by an overhead camshaft. Before coming to work at Ariel, Turner ran his own motorcycle shop and even went so far as designing and building his own overhead-cam 350-cc motorcycle. Perhaps the lessons learned building that single-cylinder machine made it easier to help in the design of the Ariel Red Hunter bikes, a series of respected and durable singles that sold well for many years.

Early in 1936, Jack Sangster agreed to buy the Triumph Engineering Company Ltd., essentially the two-wheeled half of the English company known for the manufacture of both cars and motorcycles.

Like the original Speed Twin and the Tiger 90 before that, this T100 uses tank-mounted gauges, light switch, and a built-in inspection light.

Perhaps the best decision Sangster made after buying Triumph was to appoint Turner as both chief designer and general manager of the new company. Turner's design talents were well known at the time, though his management abilities might best be described as a large question mark. The appointment, however, proved to be a brilliant move.

The first directive from Sangster to his new manager and designer involved the existing line of single-cylinder machines. Rather than design a new motorcycle, Edward's first job was the revitalization and expansion of Triumph's current line of single-cylinder models. With what would later be called the Turner flair for design, the Triumph singles soon sparkled with additional chrome plate and bright paint. As Jack predicted, increased sales did follow close on the heels of the redesign. His redesign of the single-cylinder Triumphs was the first, and certainly not the last, success Edward Turner would enjoy while working for Triumph.

By late 1936, Triumph needed an entirely new engine, one with more power and less vibration than the largest of the thumping singles. An engine lighter than a single— something that would fit into an existing Triumph frame and thus eliminate the need to design a new engine and a new frame.

Ed Turner's crowning achievement, the one creation he will always be remembered for, is the engine that came to be known as the Speed Twin. It powered Triumph Motorcycles to the top of the sales charts and ensured over 30 years of financial success.

Turner's Twin

Twenty-six horsepower might not sound like much today, but in 1937, the year the Speed Twin was introduced, many competition machines didn't even have that much power. At a time when the American V-twins, Indian and Harley-Davidson, manufactured bikes weighing over 500 pounds, the welterweight Triumph tipped the scales at only 365

pounds, but had equal or more power. Like a two-wheeled Buick, the Indians and Harleys of the day came with big, slow-turning engines, pushing around considerable chunks of iron and steel. With a small, faster-revving engine, the Triumph was the Ford Mustang of the times—quicker to rev and easier to take through a fast series of curves.

Turner's design started with a set of vertically split cast-aluminum crankcases supporting the crank on two large ball bearings. The crankshaft itself was a three-piece affair, made up of two outside "halves" each bolted to the central flywheel. Each flat-top piston included two cutouts for the valves and connected to the crank through an I-beam alloy connecting rod. The compression, at only 7.2:1, seems mild though we have to remember that the gas available at the time left much to be desired in the octane department, especially in Europe.

Although the Speed Twin was the first mass-produced vertical twin and a revolutionary engine, it was at the same

A restored Speed Twin from 1940 with the "eight-stud" engine. The true strength of the Speed Twin lay not only in its power but in the engine's compactness. Splayed exhaust ports helped to provide adequate cooling, while one-piece cylinder assembly helped contribute to the engine's compactness.

time conventional for the day. The bore, for example, measured only 63 mm while the stroke extended a full 80 mm. The Speed Twin was, in fact, a very under-square engine of 499 cc.

To keep the engine compact, the twin cylinders were cast in one piece. Likewise the head, another one-piece casting. Although aluminum alloys would be used in later years, the original engines used cast iron for both the cylinders and the cylinder-head assembly. Studs secured the base of the cylinder assembly to the cases. The first of the Speed Twins used only six studs, a number that proved inadequate and was later increased to eight.

Setting the pattern for nearly all the Triumph twins to follow, Turner designed his new engine with splayed exhaust pipes exiting at the front of the engine for maximum cooling. On the other side of the head, parallel intake runners met a simple

intake manifold that made it possible to feed two cylinders with one carburetor.

Turner's new design used two camshafts, one in front of the cylinders and one behind, set high in the crankcase and driven by a gear train on the engine's right side. By keeping the camshafts mounted high in the crankcase, Turner kept the weight and mass of the valve train to a minimum, while the position of the pushrods between the cylinders helped to keep the engine size nice and compact.

Like Henry Ford, Edward Turner liked to minimize the number of parts each machine required. Thus the timing gears on the end of each camshaft and the camshafts themselves (at least for the Speed Twin) are identical. Twin coil springs hold each valve against the seat while adjustment is provided at the pushrod end of each rocker arm. Access is provided to the valve adjustment through the threaded caps located on the alloy rocker boxes.

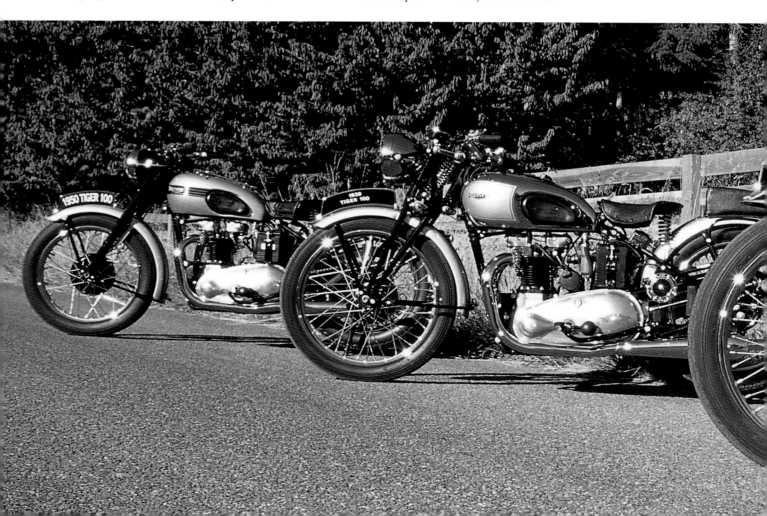

A single Amal Type 6 Carburetor with a whopping 15/16-inch bore feeds fuel and air to each cylinder through a small intake manifold. Spark is generated by a Lucas magdyno driven from the gear train on the engine's right side.

Twenty-six horsepower doesn't require a tremendously stout primary drive, so only a single-row primary chain was used between the engine and the separate four-speed transmission. The primary cover Turner designed is a simple affair made of aluminum with a small dimple necessary to clear the end of the crankshaft.

Much of the beauty of this new engine lay in its ability to fit easily into the existing Triumph frame. Thus the "new" Speed Twin motorcycle was in essence a new engine in an old frame, the same frame used for the top-of-the-line Triumph single, the Tiger 90. Like the Tiger 90, the early Speed Twins used a girder fork and 20-inch front wheel. From

the steering neck, a single top tube led back to the seat post while a pair of tubes ran down from the neck to wrap under and support the engine and transmission. The back of the frame was, of course, rigid and supported a 19-inch wheel wrapped with a 3.50-inch tire.

Looking back on Triumph's new Speed Twin, it's easy to see the bike as a new engine in an old frame. A shrewd marketer as well as an engineer, Turner took pains to ensure that no one else made that same connection. The success or failure of a product often relies as much on the packaging as on the product itself. No one understood that concept better than the genius of both marketing and engineering, Edward Turner. While Triumph's range of singles came primarily in black and silver, the first Speed Twins were painted Amaranth red. Rims and gas tank were chrome plated, with red used in the center of the rim and on panels on either side of

Still the top performance bike of the Triumph line, the postwar T100 differed from the earlier models with the addition of the hydraulic fork and stylish headlight nacelle.

Opposite: The new headlight nacelle allowed Triumph to further modernize the bikes by moving the gauges from the tank to the headlight housing. The new gas tank wrapped around the front of the seat, and included another signature item—the tank-mounted parcel grid.

16

the tank. With a chrome headlight housing and exhaust pipes, and many bright aluminum parts on the engine, the bike was a stunning visual achievement.

The combination of light weight and relatively high horsepower levels made for a very fast motorcycle, especially as judged by the standards of the day. A nimble machine to ride, a good Speed Twin would run at over 90 miles per hour. Fast indeed for 1937!

Introduced in late 1937 as a 1938 model, the Speed Twin sold well and experienced few teething troubles in its first year of service. One of the few "recalls" involved broken cylinder-to-case studs. Today the early Speed Twins are known as "six-stud" engines while 1939 and later models are known as "eight-stud" engines to reflect the additional studs added for the 1939 model year.

For 1939, Triumph had more to shout about than just a few extra cylinder studs. By increasing the compression ratio of the Speed Twin to 8:1, and porting the head, the horsepower was raised sufficiently to push the bike's top speed all the way to 100 miles per hour. In typical Turner fashion, the new sport model earned the name Tiger 100. By providing recesses at the back of the Tiger's gas tank, Turner allowed the rider to tuck his or her knees in out of the wind and achieve a closer communion with the motorcycle. He also created the signature tank shape that Triumphs would use in various forms right

up to the end of the line. To further separate the two bikes, the Tigers were painted in silver instead of red, and used innovative mufflers with end caps that could be removed to create an instant tapered megaphone.

World War II Intervenes

Further development of either the Speed Twin or the Tiger 100 slowed considerably when the plant was converted to wartime production. All activity at the plant stopped in November 1940, when the Triumph facility was leveled during a German bombing raid. By moving any salvageable tooling and material to temporary facilities, Triumph continued to produce bikes, but only the more mundane mounts needed by the military. By the time the war ended, the company was in new facilities in Meriden, outside Coventry, England. With hostilities ceased, Triumph was faced with the dire need to produce and to export. Many raw materials were rationed to industry and in order to qualify for those materials, English companies had to export a certain percentage of their production.

Selling Triumphs in the States wasn't too hard. Post-World War II America was full of young ex-GIs, sailors, and airmen anxious to buy motorcycles. And many of them were now familiar with "foreign" products from overseas, things such as the twin-cylinder motorcycles from Triumph.

This postwar T100 is a transitional bike with the new hydraulic fork and the old gas tank. The pivoting seat and sprung hub served to isolate the rider from the rough roads of the day. By 1948 the T100 no longer used mufflers with removable end caps.

The original Speed Twin engine displaces 500 cc. The T100 used the same displacement and came with an additional 8 horsepower. Triumph obtained the extra horses in standard fashion, with a larger Amal carburetor, a ported head, and higher compression.

Building a Road Racer from a Generator

To digress for a moment, one of Triumph's military products was a generator designed to recharge the batteries on large bombers while they sat on the ground. Although based on the standard 500-cc Triumph twin engine, the generators used a top end cast in aluminum to reduce the total weight.

The first savvy tuner to combine the durable, stock 500-cc bottom end with the light alloy top end was a certain Freddie Clarke, head of Triumph's experimental department. Astride a stripped T100 equipped with the "generator" top end, Freddie won the 1946 Senior Manx Grand Prix.

Yet, instead of earning a raise for winning the race, Freddie received an ass-chewing from Edward Turner. Clarke had broken Ed Turner's infamous no-factory-racing rule. Which is not to say Freddie's Grand Prix was the last use of a stock lower end and generator top end. In fact, Triumph went on to actually sell limited numbers of the Grand Prix model, based very much on the one-off machine that won the Manx Grand Prix.

The best-known use of the Generator twins, however, happened not on the asphalt of a racetrack or road course, but on the dirt of a Trials course.

Trophy Winner

Although the official factory policy was "no racing," Turner took a different attitude toward Trials and off-road events. These he felt, offered an opportunity to exhibit the durability of the Triumph marque. An additional incentive was offered by Britain's Ministry of Supply, the people in charge of rationing materials to English industry. The Ministry saw a win in the International Six Days Trials as an opportunity to show off the superiority of English products, all of which would help drive the exports they needed so badly to survive. Toward this end, the arbiters of raw materials offered Triumph additional materials to build the bikes, and more of the same if the bikes were to win.

Thus Henry Vale, Triumph's off-road expert, received considerably more support than Freddie when it came time to construct some very special Trials machines. The occasion was the upcoming 1948 International Six Days Trials, to be held in San Remo, Italy.

Triumph had no off-road bikes in the line at the time and Vale did the only logical thing. He converted a small group of Speed Twins into off-road competition machines.

With a limited amount of time, the conversion consisted of stripping the bikes of unnecessary components, installation of Trials tires, and finally, fitting the generator cylinder and head assemblies onto the stock Speed Twin crankcases.

In 1948 the Triumph team enjoyed tremendous success at the International Six Days Trial. Not only did they win three gold medals, they won the team trophy as well.

Never one to miss a sales opportunity, by late 1948 Turner had the factory producing a new model, the 500-cc Trophy. Like the ISDT winner, the new bike used a generator top end and Trials tires. Unlike those hastily constructed prototypes, however, the official bike came with a much shorter wheelbase, which made it a better competition machine than the original works specials on which it was based.

Postwar Triumphs

Most young American men wanted power, power, and more power (some things never change). The biggest bike in the Triumph line after the war displaced only 500 cc. Both the factory and the aftermarket tuners worked to increase the output of the 500-cc Triumphs throughout the late 1940s and early 1950s.

The fastest Triumphs offered for sale in the States immediately after the war were the well-known Speed Twin and the high-output Tiger 100. For the most part, these bikes were identical to the same models sold before the war. The biggest improvement in the postwar bikes was the adoption of a hydraulically damped telescopic front fork in place of the girder design. The new fork offered a better ride, more travel, and reduced unsprung weight. For suspension at the other end, the Triumphs relied on the Turner-designed sprung hub, as swingarm rear suspension was still years away.

The real high-performance bikes didn't come out until a few years later. Even then, the Grand Prix was only available in very limited numbers and the Trophy was intended primarily for off-road work. With

Note the rectangular shape of the cylinder barrels and the undrilled bosses where the cooling shrouding was attached for generator use. The development of the TR5 continued through the 1950s, first with a new "fine-pitch fin" engine in 1951, then with true rear suspension in 1954, and finally with a 650 engine in 1956 when the first TR6 was offered for sale. *Mark Mitchell*

help from some factory hop-up kits, the output of the various Triumph models was increased, though the tuners of the day eventually came up against the limitations imposed by the 500-cc displacement of Triumph's largest twin.

A Gift from Heaven

Continual development of the 500-cc twin might be all well and good—anywhere but in America. This is the country where gearheads seem to feel "A little too much is just enough," and that "There's no substitute for cubic inches." Edward Turner, very much in tune with the American appetite for speed and size, realized very early that his 500-cc motorcycles would not long satisfy the American market, which was essential to Triumph's financial success.

As early as 1949, Turner instructed the experimental department at the Meriden

factory to build a very special T100 engine. Because the cast-iron cylinders used heavy walls, he asked that the boys in the shop try an overbore from the standard 63 mm to a full 71 mm. He also asked that the stroke be increased at the same time, but not nearly as much. Instead of the stock 80 mm, the new prototype crankshaft used a stroke of 82 mm. The new combination yielded a total displacement of 650 cc, a number that would soon resonate from Boston to Los Angeles.

The true genius of the new engine lay in its external dimensions, the same dimensions as the 500-cc machines. Thus, once again Mr. Turner produced a hot rod by slipping a 650-cc engine into a stock 500-cc frame. New models need new names. Turner is said to have taken the name Thunderbird from a motel he saw during one of his American tours.

The TR5 Trophy was built to take advantage of Triumph's win in the ISDT competition. Like those factory specials, the early TR5 bikes used a standard 500-cc bottom end with the lighter "generator" top end. This example is a first-year Trophy from 1949, part of the late Benny Bootle's collection. *Mark Mitchell*

20

In the real world, the additional 150 cc yielded nearly eight additional horsepower with the engine in a mild state of tune. Thus, in 1950 the new large-displacement Thunderbird became the high-performance bike in the Triumph line.

Evolution of the T-Bird

From that first 650-cc model, Triumph increased the number of models with the new, bigger engine. The first expansion followed a familiar pattern when in 1953 the Thunderbird was "leaned on" by the factory to produce the high-performance Tiger 110. Rather than simply boost the engine's output with better breathing, Triumph did a thorough soup-up job on their 650-cc power plant. The additional power came from the installation of the higher-lift E3134 camshaft on the inlet side, along with a bigger carburetor, an enlarged intake tract, and higher-compression pistons.

To handle the extra power and the additional internal loads, the T110 engines received a new, stronger crankshaft. Additional support came in the form of bigger journals for the connecting rods and ball-bearing support for both sides of the crank instead of just the primary side. Faster machines need better brakes, and to deal with the additional velocity of the T110, the front drum brake diameter was increased to 8 inches.

Some of the biggest news of the period came along one year later, with the introduction of the new swingarm frame on the 1954 models. Gone finally was the sprung hub; in its place Triumph offered a proper rear suspension. The conversion to the swingarm frame brought other, more subtle benefits as well. The new frame meant the stylists at Triumph now had an opportunity to clean up the lines of the bikes. The oil tank was reshaped to mirror the curvaceous toolbox housing on the other side, and a stepped and modern twin-seat was added at the same time.

By 1956, Triumph thus offered some of the fastest and most popular bikes on the street, with the powerful 650s far outselling the 500 twins. And for the new model year, the Meriden factory again responded to American tastes with yet another performance leap.

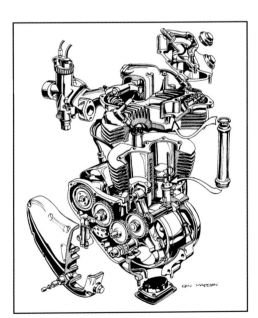

The 1957 TR6B was essentially the same as a standard TR6 from 1956, complete with the siamesed exhaust running along the bike's left side. The main difference from 1956 specifications was in the tires. The fat rear knobby measured 4.00x18 inches while the front trials universal measured 3.25x19 inches.

In Triumph nomenclature and model designations, a "C" often meant competition or off-road-only use. For 1957, however, most TR6Cs were leftover bikes from 1956 with street pipes borrowed from the Tiger line, and street tires as well. With only a speedometer, the TR6C became the entry-level TR6 model, kind of a Chevy Biscayne without a radio or heater. The TR6C model was in fact discontinued for 1958 when only the A and B types were offered for sale.

In introducing the "Slick Shift" shifter mechanism in 1958, Triumph decided to eliminate a problem no one asked them to fix. The mechanism combined the clutch and shift lever; pressure on the shift lever would release the clutch then shift the transmission. Designed as an aid to new riders, nearly all the American riders who took delivery of new bikes equipped with the Slick Shift mechanism couldn't disconnect the shifter-clutch interface fast enough.

By 1958 the Trophy-Bird had evolved into a do-it-all machine. Although many were run in western desert races and eastern TT events with great success, just as many were used as daily transportation on the street where they won many a stoplight grand prix.

Bigger changes, some more welcome than others, came in the cylinder-head department. Because of cracking between the exhaust valve seats and the mounting holes, a new head with smaller combustion chambers and smaller valves replaced the earlier head. And if the new head with the smaller valves proved too detrimental to performance, Triumph for the first time offered a twin-carb head for the 650-cc engines. The new head with the extra carburetor was offered as

an accessory for installation by the dealer or the bike's owner.

Once Triumph made the new head available for the already popular TR6, all the pieces were in place for the next big leap. The twin-carb head was the next step on the evolutionary ladder leading to Triumph's best-known motorcycle. Even if they got it wrong the first year, there is a direct link between the TR6 and Bonneville.

Bonneville, the Perfect Name
Edward Turner couldn't have picked a better name for the new twin-carb 650-cc high-performance bike. Not only did the Bonneville name ring with a certain hot-rod harmony all across the United States, it also served to remind riders that Triumph built "The World's Fastest Motorcycle." Triumph's claim to the Fastest Motorcycle title started in 1955, when Johnny Allen took the Texas Cee-Gar, a streamliner with a modified 650 Thunderbird engine, to a top speed of 193.30 miles per hour. After losing the title briefly to a factory-built NSU in 1956, Allen returned with a more powerful Jack Wilson—built engine in the Cee-Gar and ran 214.17 miles per hour. Allen's later record stood until 1962 when it was finally broken by another Triumph-powered machine.

In looking back, most of us see the Triumph Bonneville through rose-tinted glasses. We see the legendary bike as both the fastest and the most successful model ever produced at the Meriden plant. Close examination of the record, however, brings to light certain facts.

The pressure to build a twin-carb 650 had been building for some time, since the introduction of the Thunderbird. Each year it only got worse, fueled by America's insatiable appetite for horsepower. This pressure became more intense, first when the 500-cc bikes came out with a limited-production twin-carb head and then again in 1958, when the twin-carb Delta head was offered as an accessory by Triumph.

To Edward Turner and his engineers in England, the Tiger 110 was the performance king of the Triumph line. Thus it is understandable if they based the new twin-carb Bonneville on the Tiger instead of the TR6.

The first-year Bonneville uses the larger wraparound gas tank with the signature parcel grid. The side cover mimics the shape of the oil tank used on the other side, an arrangement that continued until the introduction of the unit engine.

28

The decision to build a new model was made only after considerable pressure from the company's U.S. distributors. And it came very late in the planning period for the 1959 models. Thus the factory missed the standard window for ad placement in the popular press. Promotion of what soon became Triumph's most important model might be called low key at best. A better effort was launched by the dealers through their word-of-mouth campaign.

Good News—Bad News

When the first Bonnevilles finally did hit dealer showrooms, the effects were mixed. With two carburetors hanging off the 650-cc engine, the new bike had the mechanical equipment everyone was screaming for. In the eyes of most riders, however, the package surrounding that hot-rod motor left much to be desired.

The good news centered around the "new" twin-carb engine.

The first year Bonneville used the same 650-cc engine as that used in the TR6 and T110, but with a new splayed-port version of the Delta cylinder head. Sport camshafts, a 3134 intake and 3325 exhaust, combined

with 8.5:1 compression, gave an output of 42 horsepower when used with a single Amal carburetor. When installed in the Bonneville and equipped with two 1-1/16-inch Monobloc carbs, the same engine put out five or six more horsepower.

The carburetors used on the new Bonneville came with a common remote fuel bowl attached to the seat post, an arrangement that proved less than ideal on a hard stop and was soon changed. In place of air cleaners, the new Bonneville offered only chrome-plated stacks at the outer lip of each carburetor. Other authors have suggested that the lack of air filters might have been a concession to the limited time the crew in Meriden had to design and put into production the new twin-carb Triumph.

The output of the 650 engine had been increasing since its introduction on the first Thunderbird. To keep pace with the increased output and higher rpm, the engineers at Meriden did their best to strengthen the engine's bottom end so it would withstand the additional pounding. For 1959 all 650 engines received a new one-piece forged crankshaft in place of the earlier three-piece crank.

This Bonneville uses a 6-volt Lucas generator seen at the very front of the engine, to keep the battery charged; a Lucas K2FC magneto, seen just behind the cylinder base, fires the Lodge spark plugs. With no alternator, the primary cover needs only a small bulge to clear the end of the one-piece crank.

The bad news involved the fact that the hot new Triumph didn't look very hot. At a time when the TR6 topped the sales charts and served as the bike most often converted to twin-carb status, Edward Turner and his Meriden crew styled the Bonneville like the contemporary Tiger 110. Where the TR6 used a separate headlight in a chrome housing, the new Bonneville offered Triumph's headlight nacelle with integral gauges. While the 650 Trophy offered trim, abbreviated fenders, the new bike came with fully valanced fenders ideal for a touring bike. Styling cues that might have been the rage 10 years earlier fell flat when they showed up on Triumph's new flagship.

To American buyers, Turner and his merry men missed the boat on the new 650. In trying to fathom why their flagship model came with all the wrong styling cues, it helps to look at what else was going on at Triumph at this time. This was the height of what might be called the British motorcycle industry's sheet-metal phase. Triumph, along with Norton, BSA, and others, tried to emulate the bodywork of automobiles, giving their motorcycles better weather protection and making them easier to keep clean in wet climates—primarily that of England. In 1958 many Triumphs even came with fully enclosed rear wheels,

Nicely tapered mufflers hang off the same bracket used to support the passenger pegs. No more sprung hubs, the Bonneville used Triumph's true swingarm rear suspension with Girling shocks supporting a 19-inch chrome-plated rim. The rear tire is the correct Dunlop universal.

Horsepower is what American riders wanted and horsepower is what Turner gave them. A claimed 42 to be exact, gained by hanging an additional carburetor on an already fast TR6 engine with the factory's hot cams, alloy head, and higher-compression pistons.

often referred to as "bathtubs," skirted front fenders, and metal-shrouded forks. While accepted in Britain, most American riders considered the bathtubs so hideous that dealers had to convert the bikes back to sport styling before the bikes could be sold.

Like the TR5 had successfully done, the TR6 avoided the heavy-metal blues because of its status as a competition bike. It should've been the foundation for the first-year Bonneville, had Turner not used the T110 look. But while he was known to

be stubborn, Turner wasn't stupid. For 1960, the second-year Bonneville was restyled to look like the Bonnevilles that inhabit our collective imagination. Gone were the valanced fenders and headlight nacelle. In place of the bulky touring fenders and metal fork shrouds, Triumph installed trim fenders and rubber fork gaiters borrowed from the TR6 line. And on top of the fork sat a graceful and shiny chrome headlight bucket that pointed the way toward a very bright future for the new Triumph Bonneville.

The Legend is Launched

A Bonneville Built for America

Although it took the chaps in England a full year to get it right, they finally did build the Bonneville Americans envisioned. The Bonneville that came to the States in 1960 had the curves and lines Americans were looking for, the TR6 styling that Americans expected from the start. TR6s from the late 1960s are sometimes called "single-carb Bonnevilles." That phrase could be turned around in describing the Bonneville, because starting in 1960 the two bikes came to share more and more of the major components, including the new-for-1960 frame.

Restored by Gary Chitwood for Bobby Sullivan, these two bikes illustrate the profound differences between a 1959 and a 1960 Bonneville. Different in more than just the sheet metal, the 1960 bikes used an alternator instead of the generator, which meant a larger bulge in the primary cover.

The image shows a motorcycle with a label reading "1961 TRI. T120"

Another Sullivan machine, this rare 1961 T120C uses the high pipes running along either side of the bike. Note the smaller TR6-style gas tank and "radiator grille" Triumph logo. While the C stood for competition, these bikes were street legal—unlike the later TT models.

The new "duplex" frame took its name from the twin down-tubes that ran from the steering head to the area under the engine. The new twin-tube frame replaced the single down-tube frame used on most Triumphs up to that point, including first-year Bonneville. The new frame also came with a front fork raked 2-1/2 degrees steeper than the first-year Bonneville, which served to both shorten the wheelbase and give the bike quicker steering.

Although the first frames came with only a single top tube, the design was soon reinforced. A second tube was added during the first year's production, running roughly parallel to and below the top tube in an effort to stop the frame's tendency to crack just under the steering head. This knack for self-destruction became especially apparent when the bikes were used in competition.

A big part of the sportlook, or TR6 styling, introduced with the 1960 Bonnevilles can be attributed to the smaller gas tank. Rather than bolt these new tanks directly to the frame, Triumph chose to

isolate them from the considerable shaking of the vertical-twin engine by using insulated straps and a series of cushions on the mounts so the whole affair could float on the frame.

To complement the new frame, both the Bonneville and TR6 used improved suspension at both ends. Redesigned forks provided smoother action while the rubber gaiters gave them a very sporting appearance. A chrome-plated 19-inch rim rolled between the fork legs, wrapped in a universal tire for street use and a knobby for the off-road bikes.

In back, both motorcycles used a slightly wider, though still chrome-plated, 18-inch rim. Tire choice depended, again, on whether the bike was built for on- or off-road use.

As an indication of just how little the Americans liked the styling of the first-year Bonneville, there were some left over as the calendar turned to 1960. The leftover bikes led to a somewhat confusing three-model lineup for 1960: the T120 Bonneville Super Sport (these were the leftover 1959s), the TR7A road bike, and the TR7B

34

GARY CHITWOOD INTERVIEW

Gary Chitwood is the man responsible for many of the restored Triumphs in Bobby Sullivan's collection. Along with good attention to detail and good mechanical skills, Gary exhibits great patience. Not just when he does the mechanical work itself, but also in taking the time to ensure that each finished bike is equipped with exactly the right parts. As Bobby Sullivan explains, "Gary gets it right, the right parts on the right bikes, and that's not always so easy to do."

Gary, can we start with some background on you—how you learned your trade, where you first encountered Triumphs?

"It all started around 1972 when I first went to the Bob Jones Institute, a tech school like AMI. Shortly thereafter I got into motocross racing and flat-track racing at local tracks.

"That's when I climbed aboard my first Triumph motorcycle. I was very impressed with that hopped-up 650-cc Triumph. So much so that I went out and found a basket-case 1969 Bonneville to fix up for my personal street bike. That was in 1975, about the same time that I started working at a local machine shop.

"Many of my mechanical skills come from working in a couple of different machine shops. Over the years I've learned a lot from Glenn Harding, who used to teach machine shop at one of the local colleges in Virginia. He also taught motorcycle mechanic classes around the world. Glenn taught me a lot; I've been real fortunate to get some help from him. If you had 10 of the best machinists in the country, Glenn would be in the top 5.

"Around 1984 I got serious about doing full-blown restorations. I was employed at a local printing shop at the time and did the restoration jobs in my small shop after work. As I started to do more and more restoration work on Triumphs, I bought more tools and added on to the workshop. At about the same time, I started going to some bike shows and buying parts at swap meets. Around 1989 I ran into Bobby Sullivan at Daytona during Bike Week and from there on the restoration business just exploded."

Let's talk about restoring bikes. What makes the difference between a great restoration and an OK restoration?

"To do a real nice restoration you have to really do a lot of research on that particular bike. And you need to have a plan so you know exactly how original you're going to make the machine. There's also the money issue. How much money are you going to put into this project?

"A lot of the difference is in the details. You can throw a bike together and have a so-so restoration, but a really nice restoration is correct in all the little details. A good example is the rims. If you send the rims out to be plated and the chrome shop buffs out the lettering on the rim so you can't read it, you've lost detail. So you have to do the polishing yourself or talk to the guys at the chrome shop so they're careful when they do the polishing.

"You have to have the right hardware too; the little stuff is real important. A lot of guys would go to the local hardware store for bolts, but if you're building a bike it needs to be correct. If it's a 1966 Bonnie, it's all Whitworth nuts and bolts and those bolts can be hard to find."

How do you decide which parts to use in the controversial situations? And are there times or situations where there is no real right or wrong?
"There's a lot of aftermarket stuff available. You have to do some research and find out who has the right parts. If you really want the good stuff, though, you probably want to buy NOS (new-old stock) parts if you can find them, like fenders. You can cheat and buy re-pop stuff; sometimes you have to use the aftermarket stuff. We try to do it correctly or not at all. Part of it comes down to what my customer

wants. He might want an aftermarket part. There is some really nice re-pop stuff and some that isn't right at all."

In terms of value, what is the relative value of a nice original bike versus a restored one? How does a person decide if a bike should be restored?
"If I had one that was pretty nice but the paint was a little faded, I might leave it the way it is."

What about the paint that Triumph used? Was some of that a true candy, with the silver base coats and a translucent top coat? And how do you match the original colors?
"A lot of those were candy paints, starting in about the mid-1960s. Most of those were Nitrocellulose lacquers. When we do our own paint jobs, I use RM lacquers, sometimes House of Kolor. For frames I like the Glassurit paint. In terms of getting the right color, over the years I've been fortunate to have some NOS gas tanks that weren't faded so the colors are the true colors. I could take those to my paint supplier, who took a lot of time to mix up paint that would be a nearly perfect match. Some of those original colors are pretty plain Jane colors; they aren't that hard to match.

"The hard ones to match are when you get up to '68, '69, and '70. Some of those call for a silver base and you were doing candy red over that. You didn't know how many coats of candy will give the correct color unless you've done it before, so it takes experience. We've been lucky to get good color matches over the years and then I keep notes as to how we accomplished that particular color. People are saying some of the bikes are over-restored, but it's hard to avoid. The paint, for example, is so much better today you simply get a better-looking paint job."

Can a person of modest mechanical skill do his or her own restoration in a home shop?
"Yes, they probably can. If you want to do one particular bike, there are some people you

could call for help. If you want to do it as a business, though, it's much harder to get to the point where each one you build is really right. You have to have the passion and the love of it; you can't just do it for the money. People who do it expecting to make a lot of money burn out right away."

What are the tasks that might typically be farmed out to specialists, things like the engine overhaul and paint?
"It's not that hard to do a motor, but some guys might want to farm that out. A lot of guys will farm out the paint and do everything else."

How does an owner find a reputable specialist to do all or part of a restoration?
"You have to just ask around, find out who's doing what, who you can trust. If they come to me and want to restore the bike, I would take the extra mile to make sure the motor is up to date and current. Gas is a big problem; you have to tune the engine to accommodate the gas that we have today. I would do some head work. New seats, thermal-coated valves for intake and exhaust, and new valve guides.

"I recommend the use of new carburetors; at least change the slide and needles. I like to be sure it has the right jetting. You can buy new Amal Monoblocs and new Concentrics, too, and it's less hassle in the long run."

Do you retain the points ignition when you do a restoration? Does it depend on how the bike will be used?
"Yes, I keep the points for my own bikes. But if the customer wants electronic ignition, I would install a Boyer or one of those. With or without the electronic ignition, there's no reason you couldn't ride one of these on a daily basis."

How do you minimize vibration in the bikes you build?
"Triumph never came up with a good solution to their vibration problem. The vibration will

be there regardless. I try to work on the suspension so you always have a good suspension under you that just makes the bike much more pleasant to ride. And I make sure the bars are mounted correctly. They mount in elastic bushings and new ones are available but some are better than others. In some cases I've even made my own. Little things like that help to make the bike a good daily driver."

How effective are the brakes in modern terms? How do they work in daily use?
"The shoes that you buy today use bonded linings, instead of the stock riveted linings. These shoes work better than what Triumph originally installed. When you do a restoration, you need to work with the brakes to get everything adjusted just right. They aren't as good as discs, but you can make them good enough that you're comfortable with the brakes and the way they work. Even the earlier brakes from the mid-'60s will work OK."

How fast is the value of these bikes increasing, and which ones are increasing the most?
"They are all going up, but ultimately it depends on the originality of the bike. If you were fortunate enough to find one in the crate from the mid-1960s, there would be no way to determine the value, and it's obviously going to be worth more than one that's freshly restored.

"Anything from 1963 to 1970, TR6 or Bonneville, is a very desirable bike to have. The pre-unit bikes are desirable too, but they require more maintenance than the 1963 and later bikes. And parts can be harder to find for pre-unit."

What are the mistakes people make in buying and restoring these bikes?
"If they just want a British mount and don't have a clue, the best thing to do is to call people who have been in the business.

"You can get hurt; you can get hurt badly, if you don't know what you're buying. I stay away from auctions. There are some good bikes at auction but you need someone with you who knows what they are looking at. It's probably better to buy from a private party or a specialist.

"I've gone out with people as a consultant, to look over a bike and make sure that it's the bike the seller says it is. If you are buying it at an auction, you're at the mercy of the person running the auction and he can only tell you what the seller told him."

This very immaculate 1962 TR6SS was purchased by Jim Hess from the original owner's estate. "Everything is original," explains Jim. "Except the rubber parts. The bike was so nice, with only 11,000 original miles, that I took it to Kenny Dreer for a full restoration."

street-scrambler. While the T120 Bonneville Super Sport offered the nacelled Tiger look of 1959, the A and B bikes were really twin-carb TR6 machines. To make things even more confusing, all the Bonnevilles had their engines stamped with the T120 prefix. As authors Lindsay Brooke and David Gaylin point out in their *Triumph Motorcycles in America* book, the U.S. Bonnevilles officially reverted back to the T120R and T120C codes in 1961. The TR7 badge was gone until the 750-cc twins appeared in 1973.

The street version of both bikes, the TR6A and TR7A, used a matching tachometer and speedometer mounted to a common plate, while scrambler models of both bikes used only a speedometer. Most of the 650 twins imported to the States used high handlebars while the same bike sold in the English or European markets used lower bars, what we might call drag bars. American TR6s and TR7s all used clutch and brake levers with the big chrome ball-end.

If there was one part of the 1959 bikes that did work, it was the engine. For 1960 both the TR6 and TR7 (Bonneville) used a 650-cc engine little changed from the preceding year. The main difference, other than in the number of carburetors, was in

the finish applied to the cylinders. The 1960 Bonneville came with the cast-iron cylinder assembly painted black, while the TR6 barrels continued to be painted silver (as they had been since 1956), to make them match the finish of the aluminum head.

For 1960 both the Bonnie and TR6 eliminated the generator, driven by the right-side gear train. In place of the generator, both models offered a modern alternator hidden under the primary cover and driven directly by the left side of the crankshaft.

A weak spot on the first-year Bonneville was the external float bowl used to feed both Amal carburetors. Despite a variety of mounting schemes, the float bowl allowed the engine to starve on a quick stop. If that weren't enough, engine vibration often set the float bowl buzzing, which turned the liquid fuel into a milk shake of gas and air. Midway through the production for 1960, Triumph solved the problem by switching all the Bonnevilles to twin Amal Monobloc carbs with integral float bowls.

The exhaust systems used during this period are another example of parts that were shared between the two high-performance 650 models. What we think of as standard

continued on page 47

A close look at the engine's left side shows the pre-unit primary cover with the larger bulge needed to provide clearance for the alternator. In 1962 the Lucas magneto was still used and above that a single Amal carburetor with integral float bowl.

This 1962 TR6SS did not come with a tachometer, thus the timing cover has no provision for a tachometer drive. The cast-iron cylinder is painted black. Note the cast connectors between the fins designed to prevent the fins from buzzing at certain rpms.

The C-model Bonneville was the "Scrambler" model, the closest thing Triumph had to a true off-road 650 until the introduction of the TT bikes in 1963.

Technically, this 1961 C model Bonneville should not have the tachometer driven off the exhaust camshaft on the right side. With the introduction of the unit engine and transmission, the camshaft drive was moved to the engine's left side.

This early competition model shares most of its components with the road-going Bonneville, including the rubber-mounted sport gas tank and the quick-detach headlight.

Triumph's factory at Meriden shipped bikes to all the major countries in the world. Many of those riders had different tastes and actually preferred the protection afforded by the fully valanced front fender and partially enclosed rear wheel.

The "bathtub" Triumphs, such as this very clean 1961 Tiger 110, were not at all popular on this side of the Atlantic. Most were converted to standard sport styling with TR6 or Bonneville sheet metal, making bikes like this very rare today.

A study in contrasts, a rare 1963 Thunderbird belonging to Bobby Jones, with the bikini version of the sheet metal so disliked by American enthusiasts. Behind the T-Bird a proper American Triumph, a 1963 Bonneville. Both bikes restored by Gary Chitwood.

Shrouded in mist, a gold-and-white 1964 Bonneville, restored by Gary Chitwood for Bobby Sullivan, complete with the unit engine and transmission. Air cleaners for the Bonnie arrived in late 1963.

The right side of the 1964 Bonneville shows the generally sanitized appearance of the unit construction bikes based on the new non-duplex frame. The oil tank now has the appearance of a side cover.

This 1965 Bonneville uses Pacific blue over silver to create one of the better-looking Triumphs from the period.

Although we tend to think of the single-carb 650 as a TR6, these baby Bonnevilles were also known as Trophys. This TR6R model from 1965 came with both a speedo and a tachometer, and the larger taillight assembly first seen in 1965.

The year 1963 marked the first year for Triumph's unitized engine and transmission. One of the most obvious external changes is the stylized Triumph logo seen on the new primary cover.

Although they look very much like the same parts on the pre-unit engine, both the cylinder and the head castings were new for 1963. New cylinder heads used one additional attachment stud, making it a "nine-stud" casting.

Continued from page 38

Bonneville pipes are actually the "low" or street pipes combined with low-restriction mufflers, used on both the TR7A and TR6A. The scrambler version of both bikes used high pipes that ran along either side just above the primary cover on the left and the gear-case cover on the right. Siamesed pipes were not used on American-bound Bonnevilles or TR6s during this period.

Slows the Pace of Change

The 1961 Bonnie and TR6 changed only in an evolutionary sense from the bikes introduced with so many changes one year earlier. The 1961 frame was essentially the same duplex model used one year before, though the fork angle was changed again and made two degrees steeper than that used on the 1960 bikes. In an effort to improve brake performance, both the front and rear brakes came with new backing plates with full-floating shoes.

The 650 engine used in 1961 was unchanged in all but a few details. A row of horizontal reinforcements were cast into the head, between the fins on either side, in order to eliminate the harmonic buzz that sometimes came from a series of fins all vibrating at the same high frequency. The balance tube used between the two carburetors to improve low-speed operation, introduced as a midyear change in 1960, continued. Alternator output was reduced in 1961 in order to eliminate what U.S. Triumph historian and author David Gaylin calls an "epidemic of light bulb failures."

In typical Triumph fashion, the 1961 bikes used their own unique colors. Bonnevilles came with a tank painted Sky Blue above and Silver Sheen below, while the TR6 bikes used a deep and lustrous Ruby Red on top and silver below. Part of the brilliance of those early colors came from Triumph's decision to use the silver

paint as a base coat under the main color. This early use of a base coat to brighten the top coat is what we call a "candy color" today, a good way to add brilliance to a color by using a bright white or silver color underneath.

Designations became less confusing in 1961, as all the Bonnevilles used the prefix T120 for identification. The road version of the Bonneville became the T120R while the scrambler model became the T120C. The C would continue to indicate the off-road Bonneville until the TT designations came to be used in 1963.

The last year (1962) for the Duplex frame and the non-unit engine and transmission saw only subtle refinement of both the Bonneville and TR6 models. Rome wasn't built in a day and it took time for a relatively small company such as Triumph to make substantial improvements in their product.

Although riders and dealers in the States saw minimal changes to either the TR6 or Bonneville in 1962, the engineers and planners in England were working at a fever pitch. The reason for all the behind-the-scenes work wasn't apparent in 1962. In fact, to look at the changes introduced on the 1962 models it appeared that the designers took a year off. Only when the new models were released to the world in 1963 would dealers and enthusiasts understand what the engineers and designers in England had been working on during 1962.

A Fully Modern Bonnie

One of Triumph's biggest leaps forward came in 1963. The bikes looked very similar to those produced just one year earlier, but were new motorcycles from one end to the other. The displacement remained 650 cc and the transmission a four-speed, but now the two components were combined into one stylish and compact assembly. Not content to simply introduce a new unitized power plant and transmission, Triumph brought out a totally new frame the same year.

The smaller Triumph twins had gained a unitized engine and transmission as early as 1958, and not long after the company began considering the unit design for its bigger twins. The decision to introduce a new frame at the same time may have been necessitated by the failures of the Duplex design used from 1960 to 1962.

Converting the 650-cc engine to unit construction was done in such a way that the power plant looked very much like the earlier engine and used many of the same parts. Essentially, the engineers used new castings to extend the left-side engine crankcase back until it formed the inside of the primary housing and part of the transmission housing. The right-side crankcase supported the crank and camshafts, and formed much of the actual transmission case. Although the new engine used a right-side timing gear cover that looked much like the pre-unit covers, the right-side transmission cover extended farther forward to meet and blend with the engine cover. The nice fit between the two right-side covers served to amplify the "unit" appearance of the new 650.

The four-speed transmission used two shafts, one behind the other, to contain the four separate gears. Support for the two shafts came from the inside of the left-side crankcase and the transmission's own support housing on the right side. The redesign of the engine gave the engineers and stylists a chance to make a number of significant changes. The outer primary, for example, was redesigned to include the stylized Triumph logo that many of us associate with Triumph motorcycles.

Under the new cover, the primary chain was changed to a 3/8-inch duplex chain driving a clutch assembly with one additional plate. The new unitized engine no longer used a magneto for ignition, and instead housed two sets of points under a small cover on the right side. The location made it easy to drive the ignition cam with the exhaust camshaft. The only fly in the ointment was the tachometer drive. Formerly driven off the right side of the exhaust camshaft, the new points housing made it necessary to drive the tachometer from the left side of the same exhaust camshaft.

Much of the engine's top end carried over from the pre-unit 1962 engines as well. The 8.5:1 pistons were still contained in the standard cast-iron cylinder assembly. On top of the cylinders the head for 1963 was a totally new piece, however. By spreading apart the holes for the mounting bolts, the head became thicker around the valve seats, done primarily to minimize cracking in that area. The new head also featured a ninth mounting hole between the cylinders for better overall sealing. On top of the new head sat new rocker boxes with horizontal fins to better match the style of the head and cylinder. To prevent the inspection caps from unscrewing, spring-loaded fingers were now mounted up against the serrated edge of the caps.

The position of the camshafts in the new unit engine did not change and retained their locations just ahead and behind the crankshaft, right where Triumph twins have always positioned them. Both the Bonneville and TR6 used E4819 intake and 4855 exhaust camshafts for 1963.

Similar to the earlier crankshaft, the 1963 crank was lightened by nearly three pounds and modified to mate up with a new right-side seal. The Amal carburetors used for 1963 matched those used one year earlier, though for the first time the Bonneville received factory air cleaners, introduced in midyear.

The New Chassis
Duplex frames, the source of many a warranty claim and pissed-off Triumph owner, were eliminated and replaced with an entirely new chassis in 1963. In some ways similar to the pre-duplex design, the new assembly used a single down-tube that

Although the new engine appeared very similar to the old one on the outside, internally the 650 was much modernized. Under the new primary cover ran a 3/8-inch duplex chain. Camshafts were new as well; both the TR6 and Bonneville used a 4819 intake and 4855 exhaust. The exhaust cam still drove the tachometer, though now the drive came off the left side of the engine.

split near the bottom to form a two-tube cradle under the engine and transmission. The top tube ran back from the neck to the area under the seat where it turned down to meet the cradle under the bottom of the engine. The new frame used heavier-wall tubing than that used in the past and a heavier casting for the neck. The new neck used the relatively steep rake angle from 1962. Under the top tube ran a second tube from the neck casting back to the top tube, which helped to reinforce the frame by forming an upper triangle.

While the 1963 frame was all new, some of the suspension components were the same as, or similar to, those used with the duplex chassis. The front forks, for example, were very similar to those used earlier, though they were clamped in place with new triple trees. The handlebars changed in 1963 as well. The new bars were made from tubing only 7/8 inch in diameter instead of the 1-inch tubing used earlier.

In order to further strengthen the frame, a pair of plates were used on either side at the rear of the engine. These plates tied together the back of the engine, the main frame, and the rear subframe.

Rather than fix things that weren't broken, the typical Triumph gas-tank shape was retained for 1963 though the mounting system was changed again so less vibration would be transferred to the tank. The use of a new frame did allow the engineers to change the oil tank to a more sleek and modern design. The filler cap was now hidden under the seat so the tank took on the smooth look of a side cover rather than an oil tank. The left side of the "tank" is in fact just a side cover and a convenient place to put the battery, the ignition, and lighting switches. Rubber bushings used at all the tank mounting points served to isolate the tank and left-side cover from vibration.

The electrical system remained at 6 volts though the new "energy transfer" alternator (often abbreviate ET) contained a separate set of windings intended to produce enough energy to fire the ignition even with a dead battery. The 7-inch headlight remained, though it was no longer easily detached and the housing contained a 2-inch ammeter and no switches.

U.S.-spec Bonnevilles manufactured in 1963 carried the designation T120R or T120C, for road or competition respectively. TR6 bikes carried similar labels: TR6SS, TR6SR, and TR6SC. In addition, a TR6C special was available in the Western states as well.

Considered as a whole, the new unitized engine and transmission, combined with the new frame, made for a much more sophisticated package. In place of a separate transmission and engine, the new bikes offered a seamless power plant. Where the rather old-fashioned oil tank once resided, the new bike offered a smooth, slick side cover. Instead of the previous simple, outer primary cover, the new bike presented a very stylish cast-aluminum cover with the Triumph logo. The new motorcycles moved the bike down the road in a design sense while retaining the important Triumph styling cues.

Less mechanical than pre-unit Triumphs, the new bike still used the right gas tank with a chrome package grid, a single headlight in a chrome shell, and a sweeping-R logo on the tank. More than anything else, however, it was the overall lines and proportions of the new machine that said TRIUMPH better than all the lights in Times Square.

Differences Between East and West

Although there were differences in the East and West Coast bikes, especially off-road TR6s, by 1964 those differences were significant enough to warrant the publication of a supplemental parts book, notes David Gaylin in his *Triumph Motorcycle Restoration Guide.* As before, the T120R and TR6SR models shared most of their parts,

The TT's compression was lowered to 11:1 in 1965, though the engine still used the larger 1 3/16-inch carburetors. This is also the first year for the shorty TT pipes.

Not only did they develop a series of machines much loved by American riders, they also created the bikes that dominated many forms of American off-road competition for decades.

From the introduction of the new 650 Trophy in 1956, the TR6 dominated western desert and off-road racing. In those early days, the winning riders simply stripped the lights and mufflers from their stock TR6s, added a skid plate, and headed for the desert.

On the eastern TT tracks, the 650-cc Triumph twins were equally effective. In the late 1950s the TR6, Thunderbird, and Tiger 110 models all made their way to the winner's circle at such race tracks as Peoria, Illinois, or Ascot, California. With the introduction of the twin-carb Bonneville, the riders had an even more effective tool with which to thrash riders astride other English brands or on the larger-displacement Harley-Davidsons.

Twin-Carb Competition Models

Discussions of these specialized bikes often begin with the Bonneville TT Special, first manufactured in 1963. Yet as early as 1960

Triumph offered the Bonneville in three separate models. As mentioned in an earlier chapter, the 1960 T120 Bonneville Super Sport models were actually leftover bikes from 1959 with new titles. More significant in this context are the two remaining models from 1960: The TR7A road bike and the TR7B street-scrambler. The TR7B was in fact an early competition model and might be called the father of the later TT bikes. One year later, in 1961, the Bonneville came in two models, designated simply T120R and T120C. In the new, more logical model designations, the R indicated road use while the C stood for competition.

Both the 1960 TR7B and the 1961 T120C are referred to as "scrambler" models and both came with equipment and engine tuning identical to that found on the road-model Bonnevilles. Differences between these early scrambler models and the true street bikes included the deletion of the tachometer and the addition of what some people call the "C" pipes. The twin high pipes, one running on each side, are what really defined these machines as "off-road" competition

motorcycles. The wheels used on these models were identical in dimension to those used on the road model, though when delivered in "C" form they came wrapped in Trials-pattern tires instead of the standard road rubber.

The First True TT Bike

The first official TT bike came to the market in 1963. The fact that the C model Bonneville was offered alongside the TT bikes all the way to 1965, the last year for the C-model Bonneville, is an often overlooked fact. Like the pre-unit C models, the later competition models came with high pipes, no tachometer, and knobby tires.

Although the C in the model designation stood for competition, after 1963 the TT bikes represented the truly race-ready Bonnevilles. As demonstrated by Eddie Mulder at Ascot in 1965, the TT models could and would win races—right out of the factory crate. More than just a street bike with high pipes and off-road tires, the TT bike was conceived from the very beginning as a kick-ass, take-no-prisoners, two-wheeled bullet.

The original idea of building a stripped-down, hopped-up Bonneville came from Johnson Motors (JoMo), Triumph's Western U.S. distributor in Pasadena, California. If you consider a TT bike as nothing more than a bare-to-the-bone Bonneville with a special motor, then the story of the TT starts not at a track but on the Utah salt flats instead.

In 1962, Joe Dudek took his Triumph-powered streamliner to Bonneville and posted a fastest-speed record of 230.269 miles per hour, running on fuel with Bill Johnson as rider (not the same Bill Johnson who was the owner of JoMo).

The design and assembly of the engine fell to JoMo's Pete Colman, who explains: (Should this paragraph and the next be set off as an extract?)"The engine used Robbins' 9.5:1 pistons, manufactured in Los Angeles, and breathed through oversize JoMo 1 1/8-inch intake valves that seated against oversize valve seats. The cams in the Dudek record-setter were a new grind that had never been run before. I started with the JoMo #9

relied on permanent magnets to provide the magnetic field, a good kick would produce enough voltage to fire the engine without the need for a battery, which eliminated the need for both the battery and battery box.

Unlike the C-model Bonnevilles, the TT bikes came to the showroom minus headlights and taillights. Like the C-model Bonnies, the 1963 and 1964 TT bikes used long straight pipes, one positioned on each side, though a straight extension was used on the TT models in place of the muffler. The shorty downswept pipes we now associate with Triumph TT bikes didn't actually appear until 1965. Although the first bikes were shipped with stock Bonneville sprockets for a ratio of 4.84:1, the gearing was later lowered to 5.41:1.

Because the TT was in fact a stripped Bonneville, the numerous improvements made to the Bonneville from 1963 to 1967 were reflected in the TT bikes as well. Thus the TT bikes received the new fork introduced in 1964 and the slimline gas tanks in 1966.

The bikes displayed at shows and vintage events always seem to wear polished fenders in either aluminum or stainless steel. Yet the record shows us that at least some TT bikes came with painted fenders. In 1963, for example, both the steel rear fender and aluminum front fender were painted white with a gold stripe. One year later, TT bikes came to this country with two polished aluminum fenders. For 1965 and 1966, only Western bikes wore the shiny aluminum fenders (despite the fact that 1966 Bonnevilles wore stainless-steel fenders) while East Coast examples were delivered with painted fenders. During the last year of TT production, the bikes delivered to both coasts wore stainless-steel fenders.

The Numbers Game

The two magic letters, TT, were first used in 1963 in the sales literature used to describe Triumph's new competition model. Engine numbers, however, for both the TT and the

C models read T120C until 1966. As Triumph model expert David Gaylin notes, the two capital letters didn't actually show up on an engine case until partway into the year's production, which means that early 1966 TT bikes carried the simple T120C engine coding. Also of note is the fact that many of the TTs seen at shows are not what they seem. Because of the rising value of these bikes, many are Bonnevilles "restored" as TT bikes.

"People should take time to inspect that actual stamping of the TT in the engine cases" says restorer Gary Chitwood. "The factory did it with one stamp; with the counterfeit bikes the TT must be added later and the letters usually don't quite line up."

Meriden produced the legendary TT bikes only until 1967. Despite the

The early TT bikes came with parcel grids, though owners often removed the racks and closed the holes with the factory-available plugs seen here. TT models in 1963 used larger carbs than the Bonneville. Owners had to come up with their own air cleaners when running in the dirt.

In 1966, Triumph used the "eyebrow" tank badge for the first time. This Chitwood-restored bike used the correct shorty TT pipes. Note the gray hand grips, used by Triumph in 1966 only.

The rear half of this 1966 TT shows the new side cover minus any switches or holes for switches. The rear tire measures 18 inches in diameter and carries a 4.00-inch Dunlop K70.

In 1966, Triumph switched to the slim 2 1/2-gallon tank for Bonnevilles and TT bikes. The new tank came with glue-on abbreviated knee pads in place of the more substantial pads used on earlier tanks.

TT Specials were just barely civilized and intended for "off-road use only." Note the lack of a speedometer or any lighting equipment and the factory-supplied air cleaner.

This 1967 TT bike is the work of restorer Rick Brown. A painter by trade, the bike is detailed to the max and also very correct. The Aubergine (purple) and gold paint job on the gas tank is Rick's own.

popularity of the TT bikes, 1967 is the last year for true TT bikes. Plans were made for a 1968 model, but in spite of their popularity they were never produced.

The TR6-Based Bikes

Like the TT bikes, the TR6-based TR6SC was requested, designed if you will, by Johnson Motors. Unlike the TT Special, this factory-built desert sled was never delivered to the Triumph Corporation (TriCor), Triumph's factory-owned East Coast distributor.

Essentially a stripped TR6, these single-carb 650-cc off-road specials were never produced in the same volume as the TT bikes. The lower initial production numbers, combined with the fact that they tended to live short and hazardous lives, means that original versions are in very short supply today.

First produced in 1961, the TR6SC used a stock TR6 engine and transmission. Desert and various off-road racing placed a higher premium on durability than horsepower. So while the TT bikes came with hopped-up motors, the SC bikes relied on the already fast 650 vertical twin in a relatively mild state of tune. The engine in a TR6SC is identical to the single-carb engine used in standard TR6 machines. Changes from a stock TR6 included straight pipes instead of mufflers and the change to the lower 5.41:1 gear ratio. Like the TT bikes, these single-carb competitors came sans any lights, where the TT Special kept at least the tachometer, the SC machines did away with all the gauges.

In order to get the right seat profile, Rick starts with an original seat cushion. He then adds an original seat top, which he claims can be found at swap meets. Next he adds new sides made from material very close to the original and then sprays on his own logo with a computer-generated stencil and automotive paint meant for vinyl. The seat's bottom trim is sourced from a Jaguar dealer and is actually pinch-weld molding meant for a Morris Minor.

64

Triumph produced the TR6SC from 1961 to 1966, though the 1966 model was coded as TR6C. For most of those years the bikes used two straight pipes running along either side of the bike. These were in fact the same pipes used on the C model Bonnevilles and early TT bikes. The 1966 TR6C Trophy Special switched to two short pipes that ran side by side along the machine's left side, with no mufflers.

To keep the SC machines light, Triumph fitted alloy fenders and a skid plate designed to protect the engine cases from rocks, stumps, and other hazards.

If the SC bikes had a shortcoming it was in the fork angle. Some competitors found the forks a bit steep, and would add 2 to 5 degrees of additional rake, all in an effort to give the bike more stability when crashing across the brush at 80 miles per hour.

Whether running at 80 across a sand wash in California, or 70 on the back straight of a TT track in Illinois, the Triumph TR6SC and T120 TT bikes were the ones to beat for many, many years. Although they were eventually pushed aside by lighter two-stroke machines, they left

behind a legacy that's still famous today. They didn't just win races; they won at totally different types of races all across the country. It might be the only time in motorcycle history that one brand dominated so many different types of American racing.

Like most TT Specials, this one fires the plugs with help from the Triumph's Energy Transfer ignition system—which used dual points like the battery ignition bikes but without the battery. The power for the ignition came from extra windings built into the alternator. Note the stamped TT in the engine case.

This 1966 TR6C uses unusual twin pipes without mufflers running down the bike's left side. Like the TT bikes and Bonnevilles, this model uses the new-for-1966 gas tank and Triumph badge.

lucky enough to have the talent to where I was universal. I could do all of it really. There's nothing better than to go out and just spank the shit out of them. They hate it.

"First time I ever went to Peoria, everybody had all black leathers and they'd heard about the flower child from California, and here I come with my blue and white leathers riding down the track on the rear wheel. It was a gas."

Can you talk about your relationship with Bud Ekins?

"Bud was instrumental in connecting me with Triumph. My dad worked at the Bud Ekins Triumph dealership in Sherman Oaks, California, as the parts manager. We bought all our parts there, and after my first overall desert win, Bud called up the West Coast distributor, Johnson Motors, and told them they better pay attention to me. The did, and provided parts at first. Bud also is responsible for starting my career in the picture business. He gave me my first jobs riding a motorcycle in the movies.

"We've also done some racing together. Bud and I broke Honda's record riding from Tijuana

Eddie Mulder (No. 12) with Dick Hammer right alongside, both airborne at the Ascot TT track. *Walt Mahoney*

to Cabo San Lucas by eight minutes, and at the end I was pushing Bud because his bike had a broken primary chain. I looked up to Bud; he's always been my hero."

How much racing do you do now?
"I've been doing the Baja. And Scott Dunlaney and I won the San Filipe 250 in 1998. Ended up winning the Pro 30 Championship at SCORE this year. I got second last year in the Baja 1000 behind Rick Johnson, the motocross star, not bad at 55 years old. I had it won this year[1999] by an hour and fifteen minutes when the bike broke. And I won Pike's Peak last year on my Triumph."

How much different are the Triumphs that you're running now compared to what you ran before?
"Very little. My current bike weighs 285 pounds and puts out 72—-73 horsepower. Hateley and Axtel did all the development on the cams. It's equipped with Del'Orto carburetors and a Morgo cylinder. They run fast. We just updated the brakes and the tires, and thanks to Works Performance we have really nice shocks on it. It's the same chassis that I was running 20 years ago. They might have a few more horses, otherwise they haven't changed much at all."

Currently you promote and organize vintage races?
"Yes, we do a total of four or five events per year. We do the Willow Springs weekend. We do the event with Gene Romero, the only vintage Mile race. That one's at Sacramento the day after Willow. We do Chris Agajanian's Grand National event and our own West Coast Vintage Flattrack series."

What about your dirt track schools, can you talk about that?
"The schools run for two days. The first day is a basic question-and-answer session in the morning. Things like air pressure, gearing, and how to sit on the bike. After lunch I take them out and explain how they must fit the bike, so the controls are right there. We also talk about

adjusting the suspension. The second day is on the track. I send them out two or four at a time, give them some guidelines and let 'em go."

Can you talk a little bit about the way the race bikes were set up? And the differences between the desert bikes and the TT bikes, in terms of frames and motors and how the equipment varied from one kind of racing to another?
"The desert bike was a single-carburetor TR6 with 9-1/2 to 1 compression, with Scrambles cams in a stock Triumph frame with a lengthened swingarm. We would push the front end out a couple degrees, just add a little more rake. That would stop it from shaking its head when you really start hooking across the sandbars and stuff. At Red Rock one time they clocked me at 102 miles per hour off the side of a sand wash. Fast. I averaged 55 miles per hour for 120 miles. We ran the big steel tanks and the big Bates seats. I think the motorcycle weighed around 350 pounds. Big steel skid plate. That was the desert TR6C.

"Before the TT Specials came out those bikes got a lot of attention. But once the they came out with the TT special, we were down and gone. All you had to change was the exhaust pipes and install the JoMo 15 cams and you had an out-of-the-crate racer. I took a brand- new 1966 TT special out of the crate, went to Ascot, and won the 100-lap race. We just ran it wide open. It had stock valve springs that were like rolled-up coat hangers, and on the 75th lap she got a little weak. Luckily, I think Van Leeuwyen fell off, but we won the race on a box stock bike. I put a Bates seat on it. Put a 4.00, K70 Dunlop on the front and put on the big gasoline tank for a 100-lap race."

What did you use for carburetors?
"When we first really got into the 750s they were the GPs; Axtel could make those things work. On the ovals and on the TTs and stuff, we'd run the bikes with monobloc or concentric carburetors, because it was all downstairs. They had more low-end power."

Originally built in 1971, the bike Eddie Mulder calls Black Beauty is still competitive nearly 30 years later. The special Champion frame was designed by Eddie Mulder and Dick Mann, with geometry very similar to that of a 1965 Bonneville. The front forks are from Ceriani, reworked by Vintage Iron; the rear shocks come from Works Performance.

Did many of your bikes run the Trackmaster and Champion frames?

"Mine never really did. In my opinion, there was nothing better than a stock Triumph frame. All the nationals I won were on stock Triumph frames. Everything, like a Woods Rotax, is an exact copy of a stock Triumph frame. Almost anything that steers and handles is a copy. All Nixon's TTs and stuff were with a stock Triumph frames. To this day, people call up and ask where they can get a 1964 or 1965 Triumph frame."

So the Triumph twin was a good combination of frame geometry and horsepower?

"Yes, and you can't break them. The gearbox, maybe, but really the Triumphs just ran and ran and ran."

And the only competition in any of that was?

"Dirt track–wise, in class C professional, the Harley. But there's nothing else. And once they made the rule where we could run the 750s, it was all over but the shouting."

How much heavier was a Harley?

"I don't think a Harley was any heavier, actually. Harleys are good motorcycles too. They had the whole thing wrapped up. Harley just dominated until the 1960s, I guess. That's when Gary came up with that Fireball. God love Nixon because he made it work; he was the Grand National Champion on a 40-incher. And

thanks to Colman, he's the one who actually got the AMA to change to the 750-cc rule."

How fast is your current 650 relative to modern bikes?

"At Sacramento we were faster than the Harley 883s. And we did an exhibition at Pamona at the Grand National Championship. Graham, Parker, Carr, and myself. I was 3/4 of a second slower than the 750s on my Triumph. Two seconds faster than the 883s. People went ballistic."

It seems like Triumphs are as popular now as they were 30 years ago.

"Yes. If you look at all the vintage motorcycles, the Triumphs are very much in demand. If you put a Triumph, a BSA, and a Norton side by side and have 20 people standing there, 15 are going to want the Triumph. And the Triumph is going to bring a couple of thousand dollars more. A Triumph is a really good design. They're still building parts for them. Companies in England are remanufacturing most of the parts now."

Looking back over your career, do you think you have a gift? You grew up with motorcycles, but there seems to be more than that going on.

"Oh yeah. I was lucky to just find my little niche. It seemed like I could ride better than I could walk. It was a helluva lot easier. I enjoyed it. It's a great life."

Larry Palmgren at the Santa Rosa half-mile track with Eddie Mulder and Dick Mann (No. 2) in hot pursuit.
Dan Mahoney

Continued from page 69

Bill Johnson from JoMo). It didn't hurt that Dudek worked for North American Aircraft, developers of the X-15 rocket plane. Professional engineers from North American provided ideas and helped Joe with the overall shape of the new streamliner.

As mentioned in the TT chapter, Pete Colman, then an employee of JoMo, built the power plant for the bike based on a T120 engine. Pete had the engine bored slightly to bring the total displacement to 667cc. The oversize cylinders were filled with 9.5:1 pistons, while a pair of Amal carbs, modified #9 camshafts, oversize valves, and some careful massaging of the ports all worked together to provide more than adequate breathing.

Looking back, Pete recalls the engine and its experimental camshaft. "The cams in the Dudek record-setter were a new grind that had never been run before. I started with the JoMo #9 cam (which was originally an automotive grind designed to run with 3/8-inch roller tappets). Unfortunately, this cam bent pushrods and broke rocker arms. I worked with Harman and Collins and asked them to regrind the #9 ramps to be compatible with the 1-1/4-inch-radius 'R' tappets.

"As I prepared the Dudek engine the night before departure for Bonneville, I had no time to test the new grind. I delivered the engine to Dudek and told him to buy Shell gasoline at the Bonneville pump, and joked that his first practice run should be about 229 miles per hour. Then we both laughed. Yet the results were better than my wildest dreams!"

In the end the carefully designed and constructed body, combined with Pete's powerful Bonneville engine, resulted in two new records for the team in 1962: 205 miles per hour for gas and 224.57 for fuel.

Pete explains that they called that cam grind the #15 from that point on, "in honor of the records, 15 was the number of Joe's streamliner."

Gyronaut, the Best Known of the Triumph 'Liners

The next big step in the never-ending speed-record race came in 1966 when Triumph dealer Bob Leppan drove the Gyronaut X-1 to an average speed of 245.66 miles per hour, with full FIM approval this time. Designed with help from Leppan's partner Jim Bruflodt and automotive designer Alex Tremulis, Gyronaut was a much more sophisticated machine than the earlier Cee-Gar.

Some riders, such as Sonny Burres, seen here at the Castle Rock TT, preferred the lighter weight of an aftermarket frame for their Triumph-powered racers.
Dan Mahoney

This longer and more powerful streamliner used two Triumph TR6 engines set in a tubular frame equipped with center hub steering and retractable side struts.

Although the streamliner was built at a time when twin-carb Bonneville engines were readily available, Leppan's past drag-racing experience was with pre-unit 650-cc engines, and that's exactly what the team chose to run in their ultramodern two-wheeled streamliner. Each TR6 engine carried a modified alloy TR6 cylinder head equipped with two carburetors. Highlift camshafts from Harman & Collins operated 1-7/8-inch intake and 1-1/2-inch exhaust valves, working against the pressure of twin S&W springs. Compression of 12:1 came about through the use of one-off pistons from Hepolite, manufacturers of nearly all the pistons used by Triumph motorcycles for many, many years.

A big believer in aerodynamics, Alex Tremulis designed the body, from the nose to the controversial tail, and then had it fabricated in fiberglass. On their first real record attempt, the team achieved a top speed on gas of 217.624 miles per hour. A spill on the wet salt at 80 miles per hour while slowing down, combined with a high-speed wobble, meant the new gas-powered record was the only one the team would set in 1965. With the speed wobble solved and the engines tweaked for another five horsepower, the team returned in 1966 and set a new motorcycle World Speed Record of 245.667. Thus, the decal so loved by Triumph enthusiasts, "World's Fastest Motorcycle," was born

The work of Leppan, his partner Bruflodt, and Tremulis stood the test of time until 1970, when two other teams made a serious assault on the record. Before Leppan could get to Bonneville, the Harley-powered 'liner of Denis Manning and Warner Riley raised the record all the way to 265 miles per hour.

Leppan failed to regain the record, but not because the team was unprepared. For 1970 the streamliner came to the salt equipped with a more refined body powered by two 820-cc Triumph twins and ran a 264-mile-per-hour shakedown pass during preparation for the two runs that would cinch the title. Everything went according to plan on race day. With Leppan at the controls, the bike went past 270 miles per hour and was still accelerating when a piece of tubing in the front of the bike cracked. The failed tubing caused the front end to collapse and the bike become airborne. The good news is the fact that Bob Leppan did recover from his injuries. The bad news: Gyronaut never again ran on the salt.

California Desert Racing Highlights
Triumph powered more than speed run machines. The Mojave Desert in southern California was a venue where Triumph recorded some ot its greatest racing achievements. It became the winter home for motorcycle racing during the 1950s and 1960s. The Lucerne Valley in the Mojave was the location of a series of "Hare and Hound" events, scheduled by AMA District 37 Sports Committee.

Typically run on Sundays throughout the winter season, these desert races consistently attracted hundreds of competitors and a large number of spectators. One of the greatest of these desert events, the Big Bear Run, was featured in Bruce Brown's motorcycle movie *On Any Sunday,* which included some riding by movie legend Steve McQueen on his Triumph TR6.

The races were conducted on rough desert terrain, with deep sand in several of the dry river beds. Some events traversed a slippery fire road that climbed from the desert floor to Big Bear Lake in the San Bernardino Mountains. The race routes were selected by various motorcycle clubs throughout District 37. The organizing club members marked the course with small bags of white lime, and one club member became the "hare" for the fastest "hound" to catch (which seldom happened) before the checkered flag was waved at the finish line.

The race started with the riders lined up handlebar to handlebar, engines running, awaiting the starting signal—a smoke bomb that exploded about 100 yards ahead of the start line. With a roar of hundreds of horsepower, riders raced in the direction of the smoke bomb. Shortly after the start, riders watched for the white lime markers and followed them to the end of the race.

The most famous race was the Big Bear Run, first held in the mid-1920s as a street race (not a desert race). The annual event for street racers started somewhere in the San Fernando Valley, and competitors raced their Harleys, Indians, and Super Xs on the roads (such as they were) to Big Bear Lake.

It was not until the early 1950s that the Big Bear Run became a desert race. For the 1953 desert race, 447 motorcycles gathered at the start line but only 83 were able to complete the 180-mile race from Lucerne Valley to the checkered flag at the resort area of Big Bear Lake. Incredibly, riders raced

through deep snow over the last several miles! Vern Robison won the 29th Annual Big Bear Run on his Triumph Thunderbird. Other Triumph riders followed Robison to the checkered flag, with Harry Foster placing 8th, Bob Ewing 12th, and Bob Sothern 13th.

Prior to this event, desert races had been dominated by single-cylinder British motorcycles, such as AJS, Matchless, Ariel, and BSA. At this point in history, Wilbur Ceder (JoMo's general manager) and I attended a desert race, to gain firsthand insight into the reasons behind the lack of Triumph entries. We were surprised to learn that Triumph vertical twins were not thought to be good desert bikes, and very few riders had even considered the purchase of a Triumph for desert racing!

We were very impressed with the talent of Bud Ekins, a young rider who had been doing some outstanding riding on one of those "other brands"! Ekins, the owner of a

Racing under the lights, Gary Nixon and his TT Special take flight off a TT jump. *Dan Mahony*

small motorcycle repair shop in the San Fernando Valley, was offered a Triumph dealership and JoMo's support for his racing efforts on a Triumph. Bud accepted the offer, and Triumph desert racing was about to make a monumental improvement.

Ekins started riding a Triumph in Scrambles events as well as desert races. In 1955, Bud almost won the 34th Annual Big Bear Run, but crashed in a deep snowbank a short distance from the finish line. Even so, Bud's fast and brilliant riding impressed the spectators as well as other riders, and many decided the time had come for them to purchase a Triumph!

JoMo decided to introduce its new 1956 TR6 model in the January Big Bear Run and three TR6s were flown to California just in time for the event. They sponsored Bud Ekins, Bill Postel, and Arvin Cox to ride these "box-stock" Triumphs in the Big Bear, to compete against a starting entry list of 625 riders in the 150-mile race.

At the checkered flag, it was Postel (1st), Ekins (2nd), Cox (3rd), with Larry Hestor (4th) on a Triumph Thunderbird! Triumph riders had finished 1-2-3-4-7-10-13-16 and 21. Following this great victory, the Triumph TR6 was affectionately called the "Desert Sled." Triumph immediately became the bike to ride and virtually dominated desert racing for the next 10 years.

Since a large number of Triumph riders were competing in desert races at the time, I decided to form a "Triumph Pit Crew" to handle the refueling of Triumphs (and small mechanical problems) during pit stops at desert races and at the Annual Catalina Grand Prix. JoMo and various southern California Triumph dealers employees volunteered to served as Pit Crew members. JoMo supplied blue-colored vests that had been silk-screened with "Triumph Pit Crew" front and back. For desert events, I loaded two custom-built JoMo pickup trucks with special five-gallon quick-fill gas cans that had been developed for 200-mile races at

Daytona Beach, a selection of wheels (with tires mounted), and an assortment of parts with a tool chest.

We also took a large, brightly colored weather balloon attached to a spool of heavy cord and a tank of helium to fill the balloon. The balloon soared high above the Triumph pits, and could be seen by Triumph riders for several minutes before a pit stop. Fortunately, none of our competitors copied our pit crew at desert races, but a couple did so at the Catalina Grand Prix. Because of the new TR6 (and introduction of a new 500-cc TR5), plus participation by Triumph dealers in desert racing and Catalina, many riders happily switched to Triumph!

In 1957, Ekins won the Big Bear Run after a 30-mile duel with Postel, who crashed and suffered a broken collarbone. It was another great victory for TR6 riders with a 1-2-3-4-5-6-7-8-9 victory sweep against 655 riders (many were Triumph mounted). During the same year, TR6-mounted Buck Smith won the Annual "Check Chase," which was also the AMA Cross Country National Championship. This was another 1-2-4-5-6-7-9-10-11-12-13-17-22 and 25 Triumph sweep. In 1958, Triumph TR6 rider Roger White defeated 834 riders when he won the annual Big Bear Run. Bud Ekins had a 10-minute lead 10 miles from the finish but crashed in another deep snowbank and finished in 4th place. This was another 1-2-3-4-5-6-7-9-10 Triumph victory. Bud Ekins became the 1958 California State Hare & Hound Champion on his TR6, as he led another string of Triumph riders into victory lane. Triumph riders finished 1-3-4-5-7-8 and 9 in this championship event.

Surprise! Bud Ekins wins again. This time he defeated the largest-ever starting field (872 entries) as he won the Big Bear Run. Unfortunately, Bud's TR6 suffered a collapsed front wheel before his second pit stop. Even though Ekins enjoyed a 9-minute

ONE DEALER'S PERSPECTIVE:
AN INTERVIEW WITH BOB ILLINGWORTH

Bob Illingworth is former owner of WIW Triumph in Minneapolis, Minnesota, one of the world's most successful Triumph dealers in the late 1960s.

Still deeply involved in motorcycling today, Bob is the executive director of the MMRA, the Minnesota Motorcycle Riders Association, one of the most effective motorcycle rights and lobbying organizations in the country. The interview with Bob provides a little perspective on what it was like to be a Triumph dealer during both the best and the worst of times.

Bob, how did you get started as a dealer?
"I bought my first Triumph in 1964 from the local dealer, the one and only dealer in our area. Three or four weeks later one of the mufflers dropped off. I took the bike back to the dealer and he told me it was my responsibility to tighten the bolts. So I got angry and left. A few weeks later I ran into another guy with a Triumph who'd had a similar experience. This guy asked me to fix his bike so he didn't have to go back to the dealer. Well, three months later I had a garage full of Triumphs.

"So I opened a repair shop with two partners; we called it WIW Triumph. It was just this little 30- by 40-foot shop. Up to that point I had a full-time job working on the railroad, but one month after opening the shop I quit my job. My partners wouldn't quit their jobs, so really I was the sole operator. Pretty soon I bought both of them out for $115 each, which was their share of what we had in parts inventory."

How did you become a franchised dealer, and how big did your operation become?
"We continued to repair Triumphs for several years. In 1968 the sales representatives for Triumph came to the store to tell me that I was illegally using the Triumph logo. But after talking with me, they found out I had a parts department bigger than the local dealer and that I was selling more Triumphs than the dealer. I did that by buying bikes from other dealers and selling them out of our store. They made us a

Bob Illingworth, the man who took a small Triumph service shop and turned it into one of the most successful Triumph dealerships in the world, poses with one of the later oil-in-frame Bonnevilles. *Bob Illingworth collection*

franchised Triumph dealer that same year, and by 1970 WIW Triumph was the biggest Triumph dealer in the world."

Give us your perspective on the troubles Triumph began to experience in the early 1970s.
"In 1971, Triumph tried to make a motorcycle that would compete with the foreign bikes. They had a lot of slick ideas about oil in the frame. The new bikes were in fact an ugly motorcycle; they'd destroyed the look of the machine. Destroyed what they already had. As a result our sales dropped significantly. My partner at the time, Steve Ferree, and I decided that it would be a good idea if I went to England and talked to Triumph about what they were doing and how it was affecting sales.

91

This shot from the mid-1970s shows the second WIW store (there were three), the one they moved into in 1969 when they became a franchised Triumph dealer. *Bob Illingworth collection*

"This was in 1973 and I told them that if they would go back and make the 1970 models we could sell everything they made. At that time they were having their labor troubles. Triumph in England was on strike, but the workers agreed with all we had to say.

"What people were asking for was a motorcycle that looked like a 1970 Bonneville. One that was fast, handled like a dream, and started in two kicks."

You said you talked to people who worked on the line at Meriden. What was their attitude?
"I talked to a man who had pinstriped every tank on every bike for 40 years. The pride that this man felt in being a part of the marque was incredible. When I asked him about the company and the possible closing of Triumph, he started to cry."

In your opinion what was the biggest factor in Triumph's failure?
"It was the hiring of the new management that destroyed Triumph. A lot of them were Slick Willies, marketing people. They didn't have a clue what the motorcycling public wanted, how wonderful the bike was, or how simple it was. They tried to compete with the Japanese, but they didn't have the tooling or the dream, or the drive really."

You're obviously a big Triumph fan. What was it that made those bikes so special?
"I think what made Triumph so special was the devotion and sweat and soul that went into those bikes. If the new managers had gone to the factory and talked to the men and women who built them, who cared deeply about those motorcycles, they might have had a clue. But instead they panicked and destroyed themselves.

"It's a real sad, sad thing. I think about that wonderful gentlemen [the Triumph pinstriper] in a white shirt with blue cardigan sweater and snow-white hair. The pride that he felt. We don't have people like that anymore.

"If anybody had had the insight to watch the manufacturing process, where they assembled the bikes by hand… There were no robots; they assembled the frame and put wheels on it, then they rolled it to the next building, where another group of people put the engine and transmission in. The machinery was old and obsolete and yet they made a good product. The devotion of the people is what made it work."

How was the quality of the bikes through the years?
"The quality problems really started in the 1970s. They leaked oil in the 1960s but all

motorcycles leaked at the time. The Harleys leaked just as much as the Triumphs did.

"Those new bikes in 1971 had these wire supports for the headlight and the fenders. Of course the bike would vibrate and the wire would break and then the fender or the headlight would fall off.

"When we went over there we talked to Parliament as well as the management of Triumph. My plea was simple: 'Make the 1970 Bonneville again.' We promised them that if they would do that, we could sell every one they built. And we reminded them that the bikes would be cheap to build, 'because you already own the tooling, and then you can invest the profits in a proper new bike.'

"And they should have scrapped BSA earlier than they did. They were selling a lot more Triumphs than BSAs. A lot of it is that English bull-headedness. And I'm English. Nobody understood why they made two of everything. Triumph outsold BSA. BSA should have gone, but I think there were more BSA people in management."

How do you feel today, looking back on that chapter of your life?
"I'm grateful to the people in England who made this bike and gave me a chance to sell it. It was a thrilling time in my life. In spite of the pain I would not trade those experiences for anything. The whole idea of having a successful company, of doing orientation on 27 new bike owners on one morning and have them all ride off at the same time with smiles on their faces. So many highlights.

"I wasn't just a motorcycle dealer, I was a Triumph dealer. Steve and I did new things. We rode with our customers every week. Our customers were part of our life. It was like a big family, like in England. It was our life. I didn't realize how important it was on a personal level until I started selling Kawasakis. Then I became just another motorcycle dealer.

"I don't know anyone from that period who didn't just *love* what they were doing. It was special."

This is an early shot of the WIW dealership, which was originally a small service shop, about 1964.
Bob Illingworth collection

A lovely shape, both the 1968 Bonneville owned by Denny Dingman and the 1969 owned by Wendy Parson (with the fork gaiter slightly out of place) use the sexy slimline gas tank and the ignition switch located on the headlight support bracket. Wendy's scalloped paint job is one of three Bonneville paint schemes available in 1969.

For 1969 the exhaust used on the C models was changed slightly, and the new (and unpopular) grille-style heat shield was added. The "Trophy red" paint job is Rick's own. Decals are what Rick calls "the real water-transfer-type decals from England, not peel-and-stick ones."

series but eventually a single Lucas 12-volt battery was specified.

Along with the change to a 12-volt system, the new Triumphs came with a variety of changes to the lighting and electrics. Road models such as the T120R and TR6R continued to locate the light and ignition switches on the left-side panel, though the ignition switch was now a true cylinder-type lock assembly. Midway through production, a new 700-series Lucas headlight was fitted. The new chrome headlight housing contained warning lights for the high beam and the ignition, as well as an ammeter. Off-road TR6C bikes received a smaller headlight housing finished in black paint.

On the other end of the machine, the taillight assembly changed to a new polished aluminum housing that used the same taillight lens seen in years past. On TR6C and Bonneville bikes that new housing bolted to polished stainless-steel fenders. The TR6R fenders remained painted.

Bonneville Development, 1967 to 1970

Many Triumph enthusiasts thought the 1966 bikes the best Triumph ever produced. Yet, no design can stand still, and the improvement of the Bonneville and TR6 continued. With the exception of the off-road models, the tendency for the Bonnie and TR6 to share parts remained and expanded.

Power levels continued to rise with the introduction in 1967 of the E3134 racing camshafts in both the intake and exhaust sides of the parallel twin. These cams were used in both the TR6 bikes and the T120R Bonnevilles. Also shared by both the Trophy and the Bonnie were the valve sizes. Starting in 1967 both models used the "Bonneville"-size valves measuring 1-19/32 inches for intake and 1-7/16 inches for exhaust. Likewise, both models used the same 9:1 pistons, now manufactured by Hepolite instead of in-house at Meriden. Partway through the year, the Monobloc carbs were

Like other 1969 models, this TR6 uses the last version of the twin-leading-shoe front brake with the revised and much-improved cable routing system.

Although the lens was used for many years, 1968 was the first year for this housing with the mandated side reflectors. The taillight housing bolts to a stainless-steel fender.

Wayne Hamilton's over-restored Bonneville benefits from electronic ignition, Avon (instead of Dunlop) tires, aftermarket mirrors, and a blueprinted engine.

Although it looks completely stock, with the "twin scallop" paint job, the paint color doesn't really match the stock Olympic flame paint used on the original bikes.

Externally, this 650 wears a polished cylinder head, freshly painted cylinders, and bolts with nickel-plated heads. The same attention to detail was exhibited inside, where Kenny Dreer installed new pistons and rings, and all-new bearing and seals. All parts were carefully balanced before final assembly.

timing on the first cylinder in the "correct" way, and then set the timing of the second cylinder by increasing or decreasing the gap of the second set of points.

Of course, not every shade-tree mechanic possessed the skills and tools to follow the procedure outlined above, all of which contributed to Triumph's bad vibes, warranty claims, and reputation on the street.

Eventually the breaker plate assembly was modified to allow each set of points to rotate separately. This way the timing could more easily be set with precision for each cylinder, without having to change the gap.

The discussion of the 1970 Bonneville seems to dwell on the machine's shortcomings—the vibration, the broken filaments, the electrical gremlins. Something has been left out.

That something is the fact that a 1970 Bonneville is one hell of a motorcycle. Anyone looking for a restored bike, especially one they intend to ride, goes looking for a 1969 or a 1970. The 1970 Bonneville is the bike that dealers asked Triumph to remanufacture after they'd made the switch to the new oil-in-frame bikes.

After 33 years of development, the 1970 Bonneville combined the best of what was good about a Triumph twin: a unique combination of great looks, good handling, and competitive performance seldom seen in one motorcycle.

Bob Illingworth and his partner Steve Ferree, owners of the fastest growing Triumph dealership, pose with the world's fastest Triumph. *Bob Illingworth collection*

CHAPTER 7

A Radical Redesign Goes Wrong

The Oil-In-Frame Bonnevilles

The 1971 Triumph twin was the first to truly reflect the thinking of the merged BSA and Triumph operations, and the first to reflect the design input of the crew working at the now infamous Research and Development center known as Umberslade Hall. Many of the department heads at the new R&D facility in Britain were brought in from the aircraft industry and had little or no motorcycle experience. Knowledgeable Triumph and BSA employees were given lesser positions with very little authority.

Although the design team retained the vertical-twin engine and the

Draw your ideas where you can—in this case from the 25th anniversary of the reign of Queen Elizabeth II. By using a silver finish with red, white, and blue accents, the boys at the Co-Op created one very attractive special.

Like the similar T140E, the Silver Jubilee uses the new-style fork assembly with the later post-1977 front fender, though for this application the fender is painted and not plated. Note the paint detailing done to the center of the chrome-plated rims.

Triumph logo on the tank, the 1971 Triumph Bonnevilles looked very little like the Bonnevilles that stirred the heart of American motorcycle enthusiasts for so many years. During the late 1960s, Triumph could not build enough motorcycles to satisfy American demand. In spite of this fact, the new team redesigned many of the things that made a Triumph one of the most desirable two-wheeled vehicles on the streets of the United States.

Their redesign started with a new frame. Discarding the old tried-and-true frame in favor of an untried and new chassis makes no sense, unless we consider that the new frame was fully welded, was lighter than its predecessor, eliminated the separate oil tank, and was intended to accept both the Triumph and the BSA engine.

Regardless of the reasoning, problems with the new frame surfaced before it was even manufactured. Assembly workers at Triumph's Meriden plant sat idle for three months waiting for the blueprints for the new frames to arrive from Umberslade Hall. After the first frames were finally manufactured, it was discovered that the engines would not fit unless the rocker boxes were first removed. When workers installed the engines with the rocker boxes removed, they then found that there wasn't enough room remaining to install the bolts that fasten the rocker boxes in place. This in turn created the need for modified heads and rocker boxes before production could get under way. The long wait for blueprints and the need to correct all the mistakes delayed assembly of the bikes. In the end, the first of the 1971 Triumph 650 models arrived in American dealer showrooms well past the prime spring selling season. Essentially Triumph lost a full year of sales on its most popular models.

The only silver lining to the whole rocker box redesign was the fact that the cylinder head could now be torqued down without having to crush the rocker box and gasket at the same time. These

crushed gaskets were the source of oil leaks over the years.

The new frame seemed to many enthusiasts an attempt to fix something that wasn't broken. Triumphs from the late 1960s had their fair share of problems: oil leakage, vibration, and overall quality. What they didn't need was a new frame.

Despite all that, the frame itself was, at least on paper, a good design. Conceived by Stefan Bauer, one of the engineers of the Norton Commando, and influenced by the lightweight American racing frames made by

The T140 engine used a new head and rocker box arrangement with only one inspection cover on each end. By 1977 the gear shift was on the left and the brake on the right in standard American practice.

RICK BROWN: A REAL WORLD RIDER

Among vintage bike connoisseurs and assorted gearheads, the post-1971, oil-in-frame Triumph twins are always treated like the poor stepchild. Bonnevilles and TR6s built up through 1970 are considered the best of the breed, the pure machine, the real McCoy. Dissenting voices can be heard, however. At least some of the individuals who repair and ride Triumph twins feel that the last of the bikes were the best. That with a few exceptions, the Triumph twin did improve steadily from the first Speed Twin to the later 750-cc Bonnevilles and Specials.

One such believer in the later bikes is Rick Brown, who lives on the outskirts of Victoria, on Vancouver Island off the west coast of Canada. Rick and his wife share their house (not garage) with 16 Triumph motorcycles, "Although I've got four more bikes stored at a friend's place," admits Rick.

Rick lists his occupation as pinstriper and painter. The restoration of motorcycles, Triumphs in particular, seems to take up a fair amount of his time, however. Rick enjoys both the pre- and post-1971 twins, but for different reasons: "From a collector's point of view, my main interest is in the 650 twins from 1963 to 1970. But as a bike to ride and enjoy you can't beat the disc-brake 750s produced from the mid-1970s to their demise in 1983. The parts availability is good both here in North America and in the old country, and you are usually able to pick up a machine to restore at a fairly reasonable price as the more common ones aren't generally classified as highly collectible yet." Rick has owned and restored a few pre-unit Triumphs as well, but finds them somewhat hard to use as a daily fun ride due in part to the vibration and also to the cost and scarcity of the correct parts.

"I find the later oil-in-frame machines to be better riders than the older ones from the 1960s. Once you get past 1971 and 1972 of course, which are bad years. During those two years the frame design was bad. Triumph did a stupid, ignorant thing. The bikes were very tall and people got turned off to Triumphs because of that. But from 1973 on they cleaned up their act.

"Once the Co-op was producing the bikes in the mid- to late 1970s, it seemed as if there was a lot more care taken in the assembly and overall fit and finish. By reversing the brake and shift lever, it became a lot easier and less dangerous to jump off a Japanese cruiser and onto an English twin.

"The new 750 doesn't feel as stressed as the old 650 and I find that if you add a tooth to the gearbox sprocket or drop two or three teeth from the rear, the bike turns into a fairly respectable highway ride with less vibration due to the lower revs. The five-speed transmission also helps as do the disc brakes.

"The Amal carbs, well, that's another story. Those fuel mixers have been a bone of contention for a number of years and a lot of us wondered why they didn't switch to a better carb such as a Mikuni. I'm a believer in Mikuni for a bike that's a rider. The difference they make is quite outstanding, not so much for performance but for the lack of flat spots and stalling. Purists may scream at me, but they make a marked improvement in the way the bikes work."

Among all those bikes in Rick's house and shop, the one he enjoys riding the most is a slightly modified 1979 T140C Bonneville Special. "I sold my Harley Dyna recently. I wanted a lighter bike to ride and started using the 750 on a daily basis." Rick's 750 has a single-carb Tiger head and a single Mikuni carburetor. Spigot adapters were installed in the head to enable Rick to use clamp-on lower exhaust pipes and stock Bonneville mufflers. A custom rear sprocket with three fewer teeth drops the rpms a bit on the highway and the torque of the 750 is still adequate, even when riding double. "The bike has been remarkably reliable," explains Rick.

"I've got 40,000 miles on it now with only a minor oil leak. The bike requires very little fiddling to keep it on the road. The electronic ignition has never been touched, the whole bike seems to be 'Japanese reliable,' kind of scary. Of course I saved all the stock bits in case the bike is ever sold or put back to its original state.

"I've switched bikes with other riders and they remark on how well it runs compared to older English bikes they have tried. No flat spots or stalling when you come up to a light and the decent handling that these bikes have always been known for. The bike still vibrates as a vertical twin does, but not to the degree that the bikes of a few years ago did. I've built quite a few mid- to late-1970s twins for other riders with a good rate of success and strive to make them a one-kick starter, even with the points and the Amal carbs.

"A few years ago I had a 1981 Electro 750 electric start with Bing carbs and that questionable Italian gas tank. I restored it and rode it for a while, but found it to be a bit soft in the performance department. The softness is no doubt due to the CV-style carb and the EPA-mandated changes. Other than that it worked well, including the starter, which never gave any trouble for me or the new owner.

"When I let other people ride my bike they can't believe how smooth it is. It does vibrate, but compared to the late-'60s Bonnevilles it's a whole lot better. I've also built some '76, and '77s for guys and they work very well too. Those are one-kick bikes. What I really like about the later bikes are the brakes, the five-speed transmission, and the added displacement. All that makes for a great motorcycle."

The gas tank that saved Triumph after the debacle of the Umberslade twins. Although it's sans the knee pads, the shape is true to Triumph tradition—though it's tarted up a bit in this example by the royal scallop and pinstriping.

The Lockheed disc brake seen on this and many other Triumphs of similar vintage doesn't actually use a chrome-plated caliper but instead a chrome-plated cover that fits over the caliper.

Trackmaster and others, the redesign used large-diameter tubing as the backbone of the chassis. Starting at the steering head, this tube ran back to the area under the seat where it turned and ran down to the bottom of the chassis. With twin down-tubes (yes, another duplex frame) and integral rear subframe, the new frame was lighter than the single front down-tube frame that it replaced. By using the large-diameter backbone as the oil tank, the new frame was more modern as well.

In addition to the assembly-line woes, the new frame had a few other problems,

such as a seat height 3 inches taller than the frame it replaced, and new oil leaks at the bottom of the reservoir where it attached to the sump cross-member. The new frame came with new triple trees and fork assemblies as well. Gone were the rubber gaiters and the entire Triumph fork legs. In their place were new and more modern fork leg assemblies with the standard lower legs sliding on the chrome fork tubes, which were clamped in new upper and lower triple trees. Instead of old-fashioned ball bearings, the new fork pivoted on modern tapered roller bearings.

The new fork assembly supported an equally new cone-shaped hub and brake drum. Another twin-leading-shoe design, most riders deemed it less effective than the unit it replaced, the improved twin-leading-shoe Triumph design. The question asked by most enthusiasts is why Triumph went to the trouble to design a new drum brake assembly, when the Japanese were making disc front brakes standard fare on their road bikes. And despite the huge airscoop, the new front brake was prone to fading because of its poorly designed actuation.

When the Umberslade engineers set out to redesign the 650 Triumph, they didn't miss much; the new frame served as the centerpiece of a whole new look for the large-displacement Triumph twins. Compared to the old bike, the fenders on the new one might be called "bobbed." Not only did the bike come with smaller fenders, the front fender relied on small-diameter wire supports that didn't always stand up to use and abuse in the real world. Like the fender, the new headlight housing with its shallow dome relied on cheap-looking wire supports.

The gas tanks were new too, and though at first glance they seemed true to their Triumph breeding, closer inspection showed them to be fatter at the front and sans any rubber cushions for the rider's knees. And where there had been an oil tank

Built by the Co-op and owned by Ron Graham, this T140V Bonneville is totally stock except for the aftermarket (though very traditional-looking) exhaust.

With the spoked wheels and slim gas tank, this later Bonneville still looks very much like a Triumph of old, while offering the rider the advantages of a five-speed transmission and disc brakes on both ends.

on one side and a side cover on the other, the new bikes came with flat, triangular-shaped side covers on both sides.

Above the side covers stretched a slightly shorter seat without the small hump separating rider and passenger areas used on earlier seats. Like the front, the rear fender was new, with a sheet-metal taillight assembly and mounting bracket.

The rear hubs, too, were conical in shape, though the rim and tire sizes are perhaps the one thing that wasn't changed for 1971. Dunlop K70 tires were used front and rear, with a 3.25x19-inch up front and a 4.00x18-inch in back.

Although the brake and clutch levers looked at first like the ball-end units used in years past, the base for each lever also served as the housing for the new switches used on the 1971 models. No longer was there an ammeter in the headlight shell,

and the switch on the large headlamp (Bonneville and TR6R) models changed to a rotary type. TR6Cs kept the 6-inch lamp and toggle switch.

Old Engines for a New Motorcycle

Despite the fact that Triumph's U.S. distributors built the small batch of T120RT twins in 1970 to homologate the 750 for dirt track racing, the 1971 Bonnevilles and Trophys came with 650-cc engines. Other than changes to the rocker boxes and through bolts used to locate the boxes to the head, these engines are essentially the same as the 650 engines produced one year earlier. Bonnevilles continued to breath through two 30-mm Amal carburetors while TR6 models inhaled through only one.

Traditionalists didn't care much for the megaphone-style mufflers used on the new Bonnevilles, a far cry from the "bottle"

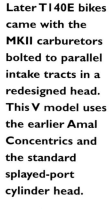

Later T140E bikes came with the MKII carburetors bolted to parallel intake tracts in a redesigned head. This V model uses the earlier Amal Concentrics and the standard splayed-port cylinder head.

mufflers used for many years on Triumphs. The TR6, offered in both R and C versions, used the same exhaust as the Bonneville on the R version. The C model had twin pipes and mufflers running along the bike's left side, complete with a slightly revised barbecue-grille heat shield.

Midway through the 1972 model year, all 650 engines received a new cylinder head and rocker box arrangement. Externally the biggest difference was the change to two inspection covers, instead of four, to provide access for valve adjustment.

Most of the bikes built for 1971 and 1972 came with the standard four-speed transmission. Midway through the 1971 year, however, a Rod Quaife—designed five-speed gearbox was made available as an option. By 1972 many of the problems introduced with the new frame were eliminated. The seat was trimmed of foam and the fork was modified, all to lower the seat height from the original 34-1/2 inches to a more acceptable 32-1/2 inches.

Midway through 1972 the frame was finally modified by repositioning the rear

sub-frame to lower the seat height a full 3 inches. This, of course, meant a redesign of all the related components, including the battery box, side covers, air filter box, coil platform, rear fender, and fender brace.

What author Lindsay Brooke called the 1972-1/2 models came to the United States looking much like "Triumphs of old." These bikes arrived complete with a teardrop-shaped 2-1/2-gallon gas tank and a proper twinseat.

Rebirth of the Bonneville

By 1973 most of the design blunders introduced in 1971 were eliminated. The Triumph Bonnie of that year began to look like a viable, competitive motorcycle once again. These were coded T140V (for the new 750-cc bikes) and T120V (for the 650-cc machines), the V standing for the five-speed transmission, which was finally made standard equipment instead of being offered as an option.

The first of the 1973 750-cc models displaced 724 cc. The engineers in England obtained this new displacement figure by

Owned by Randy Baxter, this 1979 Bonneville Special combined mostly standard T140 running gear with some pseudo-chopper details to create a good-looking bike.

increasing the bore from 71 to 75 mm while
retaining the stock 82-mm stroke. Later in
the same model year, Triumph designed a
new casting for the cylinders, one that
would accept a larger 76-mm bore. The new
bore diameter brought the total
displacement to 744 cc. This later casting
was shorter than those used earlier and used
shorter connecting rods as well, so that the
engines could once again be installed in the
frames with the rocker boxes installed.
These 750-cc Bonnevilles inhaled through
two 30-mm Amal concentric carburetors
and exhaled into two chrome exhaust pipes
and mufflers. The old signature Triumph
mufflers were long gone, and through the
1973 model year three different mufflers
were used on the Bonnevilles.

With the added power from the
additional displacement, Triumph chose to
lower the compression ratio and install
milder 71-03011 exhaust and 71-3010

intake camshafts, instead of the wilder cams
used earlier. To withstand the added loads
from the larger engine, the timing side
main bearing was enlarged, and a triplex
primary chain took the place of the earlier
duplex chain used on the 650 twins.

The suspension consisted of the new
conventional fork assembly with polished
alloy lower legs, which was shared with the
three-cylinder Trident. Clamped to the left
leg was the disc brake caliper everyone had
been waiting for. The Lockheed caliper hid
under a chrome cover and squeezed a
10-inch rotor.

With the increase in displacement the
old TR6R became the TR7RV Tiger. The
new Tiger was in fact still a Bonnie with one
less carburetor. And the high-piped TR6C
was dropped from the lineup.

The 1973 T140V and smaller brother
T120V (650-cc Bonnevilles were offered
for sale alongside the 750-cc bikes in

England and other export markets only) were good motorcycles with adequate power and pleasing aesthetics. They looked like Triumphs of old. Yet, the rebirth of the Bonneville was short lived. About the time production of the 1974 models was getting under way, new company management announced it would close the Meriden plant—part of an ill-fated scheme to rescue the failing BSA empire. The intensely loyal Triumph workers quickly went on strike and blockaded the factory. Thus few 1974 models were built, making a Bonneville a rather rare bird indeed. And by the time the strike was settled it was the spring of 1975, making any Triumphs with a 1975 title rare as well.

The few Bonnevilles and Tigers that carry a 1974 title are essentially the same as 1973 bikes, the notable exception being the use of new colors on the gas tanks. Bonnevilles (T140V) came in Cherokee red and white while the Tiger (TR7RV) came in Jade green and white. T120 Bonnevilles for other markets were still being produced at this time, and came in their own colors, purple and white.

By the time the strike was settled and the workers' Co-op established, very little time remained to produce 1975 machines.

Co-operative Triumphs
The first bikes truly produced by the new social experiment at Meriden were the 1976 models. In most respects these Bonneville and Tiger 750s are identical to the 1974 and 1975 bikes. The biggest change between pre- and post-1976 bikes is the U.S. federally mandated left-side gear change. By 1976 the T120V (650) Bonnevilles were no longer offered alongside the 750s. The other change is the one noted by Rick Brown in his real-world commentary, the addition of a rear disc brake to complement the front Lockheed installed on 1973 and later bikes.

Change came slowly to the Triumph twin during this period and the newest thing that

happened during the 1977 model year was the introduction of the limited-edition Silver Jubilee. Decked out in silver with special seat and trim, unique chrome, painted and pinstriped wheel rims, and chrome-plated engine and transmission covers, this special edition was designed and marketed to commemorate the 25 years of Queen Elizabeth's reign. Although the official literature described the production of only 1,000 of these bikes, a total of 2,400 were produced. The discrepancy is best explained if you understand that Triumph built 1,000 bikes for the English market and another 1,000 for the

Ron's black Bonneville uses the new non-gaitered hydraulic fork supporting a 19-inch spoked wheel and Lockheed disc brake.

American market, plus an additional 400 for various other markets.

In order to comply with ever-tightening EPA regulations in the United States, a major redesign of the cylinder head and intake tract was undertaken. The designation for the new model introduced in mid-1978 was T140E. Instead of continuing with the splayed intake tracts, the new model used a cylinder head with parallel intake tracts. Each of these intake ports connected to an Amal MKII Concentric carburetor, complete with an enrichment circuit.

With the new cylinder head and intake manifold in place, a larger, single Amal carburetor wouldn't fit between the intake and the airbox. This spelled the end of the TR7, son of the TR6 and the TR5 before that.

New plastic airbox covers and badges were introduced with the Jubilee in 1977 and used on all 750s from 1978 on. Other sheet-metal changes included the use of new scalloped paint schemes on T140 gas tanks. Modernization of the Bonneville continued with the introduction in 1979 of a negative-ground electrical system. Further improvements in this regard include the addition of a new electronic ignition and improved switches, both from Lucas.

Despite the Co-op's attempts at modernization and the much-improved quality, sales of Bonnevilles consistently fell short of projections. Fierce competition from more modern Japanese machines, a weak economy both in America and England, and a poor dollar-pound relationship all served to make the classic vertical twin a tough sell in dealerships across the land.

For improved sales, Triumph looked to new models, though the development of truly new models was hampered by the Co-op's acute shortage of cash.

New Models from the Co-op

In the late 1970s, America was still caught up in the waning days of the chopper craze and some of the most popular bikes on the street were the "specials" produced by various factories. Kawasaki built LTDs, Yamaha brought in its 650-cc vertical-twin Special, and Harley-Davidson built the flamed Wide Glide. Anxious to increase sales and limited by their cash shortage from doing any expensive R&D, Triumph offered its own Bonneville Special for 1979.

Technically the new model was a T140D Bonneville Special. In place of the standard spoked wheels, the new cruiser came to market with U.S.-made Lester cast wheels. And instead of the usual Triumph exhaust system, the T140D Special offered riders a two-into-one system with the muffler mounted on the bike's right side. Like any good factory chopper, the Triumph came with a wider rear tire and a king- and queen-style seat. The Bonnie Special came to market with a slim 2-1/2-gallon fuel tank and a new abbreviated tank badge.

The relationship between the American dollar and the British pound at that time meant the new Special retailed for $3,225, a lot of money in 1979. As Lindsay Brooke and David Gaylin point out in *Triumph Motorcycles in America,* "The factory had geared up for an estimated sale of 8,000 machines in the U.S. during that year (1979)." As they go on to explain, that projection proved to be "way off the mark." Both the standard T140E and T140D Special failed to sell in any significant numbers. The cost of tooling up to produce all those bikes created a severe crimp in Triumph's cash flow—a crunch from which the Co-op never really recovered.

Which is not to say this is the end of the story. If Triumph motorcycles, and the people who manufactured them, are notable for one thing it's their cat-like ability to shake off apparent death and soldier on with new ideas, models, and plans for a successful future.

Gone are the winged collars where the exhaust pipes meet the head. Note the simple tank badge, the ribbed ignition cover, and the way the head pipes flare out to the side before tucking in tight under the frame.

CHAPTER 8

The Bonneville Falls Behind

Triumph Closes Its Doors

The phrase "hope springs eternal" might have been coined at the Meriden factory. Despite an unending litany of bad news and financial disasters, Triumph soldiered on through the late 1970s and early 1980s, always with a new plan based on a new model.

Unknown to most American Triumph enthusiasts and even dealers, the beginning of the end took place about 30 years before the company's final demise. A business transaction took place in 1951 that would have huge repercussions for anyone associated with Triumph motorcycles, but not for nearly 20 years or more.

One of the last models to come out of Meriden, this T140ES Electro added an electric starter and European tank to the standard T140. By 1982, Triumph had finally converted to a negative ground electrical system and electronic ignition.

Owned by Randy Baxter, this 750 Bonnie uses the later cylinder head with parallel intake ports connected to Bing carburetors.

The transaction was the sale of Triumph Engineering Company, Ltd. to BSA. Triumph was a successful company at the time and Jack Sangster's motives are unknown. American enthusiasts remained mostly unaware of the sale. The vast majority assumed Triumph to be a separate company and that's exactly the way Triumph carried on for years and years.

The effects of the sale didn't become apparent to most dealers and members of the motorcycle industry until the middle of the 1960s when BSA began to consolidate its hold on various parts of the Triumph empire. The changes were magnified due to some major personnel changes that took place at about the same time.

The first major personnel change occurred in March of 1962, when Bill Johnson, founder of Johnson Motors, the western distributor of Triumph motorcycles, died of a heart attack. Bill's close friend and confidant, Ed Turner, retired two years

later, though he remained on the BSA Board of Directors for another three years.

The BSA Group purchased controlling interest in Johnson Motors (the eastern distributor was already factory owned) early in 1965 and soon went on to buy the western distributor for BSA motorcycles as well.

To give some idea of just how out of touch the new management was, in 1966 all the U.S. Triumph dealers were told they would have to sell BSA bikes as well, and all BSA dealers were instructed to market Triumphs. Needless to say, many Triumph staff and dealers simply quit as soon as they were told of the planned merger of the two sales networks. Author Lindsay Brooke says that the announcement caused a "near riot and almost shut down Triumph's U.S. operations."

The next major loss of personnel came in late 1969 when the four distinct American distribution companies (East and West Coast for both BSA and Triumph) were merged into one. The new corporation, BSACI, was then put under the control of a new president, Peter Thornton, a man with a background in advertising. Once again, non-motorcycle people forced former rivals to work together in merged organizations. Predictably, some key Triumph technical people left the new organization.

Overseas, the situation was even worse. At a time when Triumph needed to be working to correct oil leaks and electrical gremlins, and address the flood of small- to medium-sized machines coming in from Japan, BSA had other ideas. The parent corporation spent millions of pounds on a new research center and the development of a three-wheeled 50-cc scooter.

The first major product to come out of Umberslade Hall, BSA Group's expensive R&D facility, was the new oil-bearing frames for the group's singles and 650-cc twins. A flawed project if ever there was one, the frame appeared to be designed with no

concern for assembling the motorcycle. The Ariel 3 scooter was never manufactured in any volume. Both enterprises bled off enormous amounts of money and energy that BSA Group could ill afford to waste. Although it wasn't apparent in 1951, the sale of Triumph to BSA was the worst thing that ever happened to Triumph Motorcycles.

The transaction's consistent liggering effects lasted far into the future, and in 1980 the Triumph brand was on its last leg. For the 1980 model year, a kick starter always seemed as much a part of a Triumph motorcycle as the teardrop-shaped tank. Yet Triumph introduced the Electro, a Bonneville with an electric starter. The Electro used a Lucas starter positioned at the rear of the engine, in the spot occupied by the magneto so many years before. The starter used a sprag clutch on the drive end and connected to the engine through the timing gears. The increased electrical demands meant that this model, which wasn't sold in the

Owned by Wayne Hamilton, this TSS is documented to be the last TSS shipped to the States. It is in fact the last one to be produced.

United States until the 1981 model year, used a larger battery and battery carrier.

By combining the new electric-start Bonneville with a special paint job, Triumph created another niche model along the same theme as the earlier Silver Jubilee. This time the new model, dubbed the Bonneville Royal, honored the wedding of Prince Charles and Diana. By this time the company no longer fit teardrop-shaped tanks built in England to the Bonnevilles; thus the Royal came with the fat blob of a tank sourced from an Italian firm, combined with a stepped seat and chrome fenders.

The Royal never enjoyed even a small percentage of the success of that earlier regal special. Only 250 examples were produced and very few of those came to American shores.

Looking back at Triumph during this last painful period, you can't fault them for

The eight-valve heads started in the late 1960s as a Weslake-engineered kit designed to fit existing 650 engines. For production in 1982, the eight-valve head was combined with new matching aluminum cylinders cast in a rectangular shape with steel sleeves.

trying. If Americans failed to buy the new Triumph cruiser, maybe what they needed was a new vertical-twin touring bike. Some call the Executive touring bike Triumph's answer to BMW. With electric starting, standard fairing, and hard bags and tour pack, the upscale Executive provided both weather protection and a place to put your heavy leather jacket.

Bigger news at the time was the introduction early in 1982 of two new Triumph models. Although the TSX was a rather modest undertaking, the TSS ranks as one of the more exciting bikes ever produced at Meriden.

Looking at the TSX today, you see another "special" designed to take advantage of the American cruiser fad, by that time a trend getting a little long in the tooth. If Harleys on the street were equipped with 15-inch and 16-inch rear tires, so could the new Triumph, which used a 16-inch Avon Roadrunner in place of the standard 18-inch rubber. The TSX also included the mandatory stepped seat, a pair of short megaphone-style mufflers, bobbed fenders, and a smaller teardrop gas tank of Italian manufacture. The rest of the bike was standard-issue late-season

The Bonneville that never made it to mass production. Note the features people were crying for: Morris mag wheels, disc brakes, and electric start, all borrowed from the T140ES.

Look closely and you will see the familiar Triumph primary cover and behind that a pair of stock lower cases. Inside the cases, however, the TSS housed a totally new crank assembly with larger-diameter bearing bosses with extra webbing for support. The end result was a very stiff crankshaft that nearly eliminated Triumph's number-one bugaboo: vibration.

The big rectangular light assembly met all the DOT specifications though it certainly didn't do much for the machine's overall appearance. Note the high-quality rear shock absorbers with remote reservoirs.

Bonneville with the 750 engine, disc brakes, and five-speed transmission.

If the TSX was too little too late, the TSS offered too much—and it was still too late. Based on a Weslake Engineering cylinder head developed with help from American dealer and racer Jack Wilson, the new bike used four valves per cylinder to increase the breathing ability of Edward Turner's long-lived design. Not content to simply add horsepower, the design team went so far as to build a completely new crankshaft assembly. Produced from a single forging, the new crank used larger-diameter, narrower big-end bearings supported by

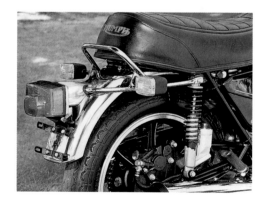

webbing on either side. Designed to be much stiffer than the standard Triumph crankshaft, the new one-piece crankshaft fit in standard Bonneville crankcases to produce what is probably the fastest, smoothest, and highest-revving Triumph ever to leave the factory.

In addition to the new crank, the TSS used a completely new cylinder casting. The new cylinders differed from the old in almost every way imaginable. Where the old cylinder barrel casting was essentially round in shape, the new one was square. Instead of widely spaced fins, the new engine used more fins spaced close together for more total cooling area. Even the bore centerlines were different, spaced 1/2 inch farther apart than on a standard 750 engine. Cast in aluminum, the new cylinder barrel relied on a steel liner to provide a durable surface for the piston rings to run against. The aluminum cylinder head matched the new cylinders with the same close-pitch fins.

Triumph's exotic new engine used camshafts positioned in the standard front and rear locations, though the valve timing was considerably different from anything seen on a two-valve Triumph. Pushrods too were close to standard issue in their dimensions and location, though each rocker arm had two fingers for depressing two valves instead of only one. Compared to a two-valve Triumph, the new head used four smaller valves set at a steeper angle around a central spark plug, located in a shallow combustion chamber. Cutouts in the flat-top pistons provided clearance for the valves while allowing for a 10:1 compression ratio. The new head included the lower half of the rocker boxes as an integral part of the casting, with two separate covers.

In Europe and the U.K., TSS models used two Amal MKII 34-mm carburetors while the same bikes shipped to the States used constant-velocity Bing fuel-air mixers. The rest of the bike was very similar to Bonnevilles of the period (T140ES) and

young engineers and created a brain trust so that now we have our own technology. This engine was developed primarily with our own resources and by our own people."

The engine Triumph developed in-house is unique to the Bonneville line. It's not part of the old modular plan, nor is it a spin-off from another of Triumph's expanding line of bikes. Visually very similar to the old engines, this new power plant is a true twin displacing just less than 800 cc. Performance- wise, Mike describes it as, "Light with plenty of torque. The one I rode was an early sample. They plan to push the torque curve down further in the rpm range. This bike has performance very much like the old Bonneville, but with more torque and less vibration."

Like Harley-Davidson, Triumph was forced by the market to retain an engine design with inherent vibration. And like Harley-Davidson, they arrived independently at the same solution: Use counterbalancers to eliminate the vibration. Just behind the new vertical twin is a new transmission. Actually, it's a transmission borrowed from one of Triumph's existing bikes. By eliminating one gear, the product planners have developed a five-speed transmission that Mike describes as a four-speed with an overdrive fifth. Chain drive moves the power to the rear wheel, which, like the front, is a spoked design.

The new vertical-twin engine and five-speed transmission bolt into a steel frame. To quote Mike Vaughan again, "The frame looks like a typical down-tube chassis, but the engine is actually a stressed member. They've hidden the oil cooler and made it look like it's a part of the frame. When you see the mock-up you'll understand."

The sheet metal is strictly 1969, right down to the knee pads at the back of the gas tank. Although the tank does share the shape of the originals, right down to the eyebrow badge, it's patterned after the larger European version instead of the slimline

tank used on American Bonnevilles from the late 1960s.

Triumph prides itself on the large percentage of each motorcycle that is manufactured in-house. Not only are the design and engineering done at the Triumph facility located in Hinckley, Leicestershire, nearly all the machining, as well as sheet metal and assembly, is done there as well. Some of the work that continues to be done through outside vendors will move inside when the new building is finished.

Although most aspects of the new bike are set in stone, there remain a few loose ends. Triumph decided not to take the nostalgia thing too far, and equipped the new bike with disc brakes. And while it seems logical to borrow a paint scheme from one of the old Bonnevilles or possibly a TR6, the paint colors are still undetermined as of 1999.

In terms of price, the new bike will be relatively inexpensive. Though the primary job of the bike is to open up a whole new nostalgia segment for Triumph, the pricing will position the bike as an entry-level machine. Essentially the bike will fit into two market niches at once.

When asked, Mike Vaughan reports that there may be at least one spin-off model based on the new Bonneville, and that one or two of the current cruisers will remain in the lineup.

So it seems that Triumph has taken the advice of Bob Illingworth from WIW Triumph. In 1973, Bob asked them to go back to building the old Bonneville. Well, they have. But instead of building the old Bonneville and using the profits to fund new models, they've done it the other way around. By building a foundation of very current machines that sell well around the world, Triumph can now afford to reintroduce our favorite model. And so what if it's taken them nearly 30 years to reach this decision. The important thing is not how long it took, but the simple fact they decided to do it—to build a new Bonneville.

Index

Agajanian, Chris, 72
Agajanian, J. C. "Aggie", 84
Allen, Johnny, 27, 68, 69
AMA, 76, 78, 80, 82, 84, 99
American TT (Tourist Trophy) Racing, 82
Ariel Motorcycles, 12
Ariel Red Hunter, 12
Ariel Square Four, 12
Ascot TT, 69, 71, 77
Bauer, Stefan, 105
Baxter, Randy, 88, 111, 118
Benolken, Mike, 21
Big Bear Run, 76–78
Bloor, John, 125–127
Bootle, Benny, 20, 24
Brooke, Lindsay, 38, 111, 115, 118
Brown, Bruce, 76
Brown, Dick, 21, 23, 53
Brown, Rick, 64, 106, 107, 113
Bruflodt, Jim, 75, 76
Brundage, Bert, 80
BSA, 90, 93, 99, 103, 105, 113, 118, 119
BSACI, 118
Burres, Sonny, 75
Butler, George, 83
Castle Rock TT, 75
Catalina Grand Prix, 78, 80
Cedar, Wilbur, 68, 70, 77
Charles, Prince of Wales, 121
Chitwood, Gary, 11, 33, 35–37, 43, 44, 54, 60–62, 89
Clark, Terry, 14
Clarke, Freddie, 18, 19
Coates, Rod, 80
Colman, Pete, 56, 60, 68, 75, 84
Copage, Dusty, 69
Cox, Arvin, 78
Davidson, Walter, 80
Daytona 995, 126
Diana, Princess of Wales, 121
Dingman, Denny, 94
Dorresteyn, Dick, 80, 81, 84, 85

Dreer, Kenny, 37
Dudek, Joe, 56, 68, 69, 75
Dudeck streamliner, 60
Dunlaney, Scott, 72
Ekins, Bud, 57–59, 71, 77, 78, 80
Elizabeth II, Queen of England, 103, 113
Evans, Ted, 82
Ewing, Bob, 77
Federation Internationale Motorcycliste (FIM), 69
Ferree, Steve, 91, 101
Fisher, Gary, 83
Foster, Harry, 77
Fulton, Walt, 82, 83
Gaylin, David, 38, 47, 50, 115
Gibson, Johnny, 80
Graham, Ron, 109
Hamel, Steve, 87
Hamilton, Wayne, 119
Hammer, Dick, 71
Hancox, Hughie, 100
Harding, Glenn, 35
Harris, Les, 123
Hateley, Jack, 85
Hawley, Don, 80
Hess, Jim, 26, 37
Hestor, Larry, 78
Hurst, Brad, 85
Illingworth, Bob, 91–93, 101, 127
International Six Days Trials, 1948, 19, 20, 24
Isle of Man TT Racing, 82
Johnson Motors, 56, 60, 64, 68, 70, 75, 78, 80–82, 84, 85, 118
Johnson, Bill, 56, 68, 69, 118
Johnson, Rick, 72
Joiner, Chuck, 85
Jones, Bobby, 43
Kretz, Ed, Sr., 70, 80, 82
Kretz, Ed, Jr., 82, 83
Leonard, Joe, 80, 84
Leppan, Bob, 75, 76
Magri, Armondo, 82
Mangham, Stormy, 68

Mann, Dick, 73, 74
Manning, Denis, 76
McKenna, Jim, 126
McQueen, Steve, 76, 80
Meier, Billy, 83
Minnesota Motorcycle Riders Association (MMRA), 91
Mulder, Eddie, 56, 58, 70–74, 80, 85
Nelson, Ron, 80
Nixon, Gary, 79, 80
On Any Sunday, 76
Palmer, Dave, 85
Palmgren, Chuck, 80, 81
Palmgren, Larry, 74, 80, 81
Parson, Wendy, 94
Payne, Sid, 85
Pearson, Bruce "Boo", 82
Philips, Jimmy, 80, 82, 83
Postel, Bill, 78
Quaife, Rod, 111
Raush, Burt, 83
Remmell, Wally, 83
Riley, Warner, 76
Robison, Vern, 77
Rockwood, Tom, 82, 85
Romero, Gene, 67, 72, 80, 82, 85
Routt, Sonny, 81, 99
Sangster, Jack, 12, 13, 118
Scott, Gary, 82, 85
Senior Manx Grand Prix, 1946, 19
Slick Shift shifter mechanism, 27
Smith, Buck, 78
Sothern, Bob, 77
Sullivan, Bobby, 11, 33–35, 44, 60, 89
Tanner, Sammy, 80
Team BSA, 82
Team Triumph, 81, 82
Texas Cee-Gar, 27, 68, 69
Thornton, Peter, 119
Tremulis, Alex, 75, 76
Triumph Corporation (TriCor), 64
Triumph Engineering Company Ltd., 12, 118

Triumph Grand Prix, 19
Triumph Motorcycles Ltd., 123
Turner, Edward, 12–16, 20, 25, 27, 28, 30, 31, 53, 90, 118, 122
Umberslade Hall, 103, 105, 108, 119
Vale, Henry, 19
Van Leeuwen, Skip, 77, 85
Vaughan, Mike, 126, 127
Williams, J. D., 80
Wilson, Jack, 68, 69, 122, 27
Wirth, Eddie, 85
WIW Triumph, 91–93, 100, 127
World War II, 16, 17

Models
650 Triumph, 108
650 Trophy, 30, 55
Adventurer, 126
Bonneville, 23, 25, 27–35, 38, 43–45, 47, 49, 50, 53, 67, 85, 87, 88, 90, 94, 99, 101, 109, 110, 112, 113, 123, 125–127
Bonneville C-model, 40, 41, 56
Bonneville Royal, 121
Bonneville Special, 1979, 111
Gyronaut X-1, 75
Silver Jubilee, 103, 104, 113, 115
Speed Triple, 126
Speed Twin, 7, 13–19, 82
Star TT, 1951, 83
T100, 11, 12, 16, 18–20, 21, 24–26, 28, 31
T120 Bonneville, 47, 80, 84, 113
T120 Bonneville Super Sport, 34, 38, 55
T120 TT, 65
T120C, 34, 38, 47, 50, 55, 61
T120R, 38, 47, 50, 55, 95

T120RT, 81, 85, 99, 110
T120V, 111
T140 Bonneville, 105, 123
T140C Bonneville Special, 1979, 106
T140D Bonneville Special, 1979, 115
T140E, 110, 115
T140ES Bonneville, 122
T140ES Electro, 117
T140V Bonneville, 109, 111–113
Thunderbird, 6, 20, 21, 24, 27, 28, 55, 68, 77, 78, 82, 83, 126
Tiger 90, 12, 14
Tiger 100, 12, 14–16, 19, 28, 30, 43, 55, 83
Tiger 100 twin, 14, 15
Tiger 110, 1961, 43
Tiger 750, 113
TR5, 24, 26, 59, 80
TR5 Trophy, 1949, 20
TR6, 23–28, 30, 33, 34, 38, 47, 49, 50, 53, 55, 59, 67, 72, 76, 78, 80, 88, 95
TR6A, 26, 38, 47
TR6B, 27
TR6C, 24, 27, 50, 54, 65, 88–90, 95, 97, 110, 111
TR6C Trophy Special, 1966, 65
TR6R, 45, 88–90, 95, 110–112
TR6SC, 50, 64, 65
TR6SR, 50
TR6SS, 37, 40, 50
TR7, 38, 115
TR7A, 34, 38, 47, 55
TR7B, 34, 55
TR7RV Tiger, 112
Triumph 500, 84
Triumph, 1979, 103
Trophy, 9, 19, 24, 25, 110
Trophy-Bird, 24, 27, 83
Trophy Special, 56
TSS, 119, 122, 123
TSX, 121
TT, 60–62, 64
TT models, 60–66
TT Special, 53, 55, 60, 63, 65, 72, 79, 84, 85